your
colours
your
home

your colours your home

decorating with the colours that
reflect your personality

Pennie Cullen

Carolyn Warrender

Frances Lincoln

To my family, Robin, Tom and Ben, for their love and support,
and to my friend Catkin for her advice, patience and loyalty.
P C

For my brother Hugh, and Bea, to celebrate their wedding.
C W

Frances Lincoln Limited 4 Torriano Mews Torriano Avenue London NW5 2RZ

Typography, design and layout © Frances Lincoln Limited 2001
Text © Pennie Cullen & Carolyn Warrender 2001
Seasonal colour palettes © Pennie Cullen & Carolyn Warrender 2001
Creating the look colour palettes © Carolyn Warrender 2001
Personality concept/colour cycle wheel © Pennie Cullen @ Growing Colour 1998

First Frances Lincoln edition: 2001

A catalogue record for this book is available from the British Library.

ISBN 0 7112 1627 4

Printed in Singapore

Contents

Preface

All too often, colour is not considered a priority when designing a home. We take colour for granted and forget that it is the key to creating successful decorating schemes. It is very easy to play safe and always use the same colours, yet in my work I often see people who are not happy with their surroundings – although they are not sure why. They may have chosen good and innovative colours, but they may well not be the right ones for them.

For many years, Johannes Itten's work on seasonal colour analysis has been the recognized method for selecting clothing based on individual colouring. Having my own colours analysed inspired a fascination with the process, and I went on to train as a colour analyst. I became convinced that if Itten's theories worked for clothes, they should also work for interior design.

Pennie Cullen and I met through a mutual love and study of colour. Pennie – a sociologist and colour consultant – believes that our colour preferences are based on our individual personalities. By understanding our responses to colour and by implementing Itten's seasonal colour analysis, she believes that we can each create our own harmonious living environment. This book has evolved from an intertwining of Pennie's colour work and personality theories with my interior design and colour analysis experience.

In reading this book, you will gain a whole new dimension in the creation of your ideal home – the use of your own, personalized colours. No two people are alike, and by discovering your colours you will see how you can live in harmony with your environment and with other people. You will also find here a guide to basic interior design, ideas about how to create individual looks and examples of past decorating styles and colours. Decorating your home should be an enjoyable and rewarding experience, and this book will set you off on an inspirational – and colourful – journey of discovery.

Carolyn Warrender.

Introduction

Colour surrounds us: we take it for granted, quite unaware
of the effect it can have on our lives, although it contains
the key to creating the home of our dreams

This book is about creating an individual style for
your home through the use of colour. By
incorporating ideas founded on personality and
colour theories with inspirational ideas about the
interior use of colour, you will discover how to
achieve a truly personal decorative style.

Johannes Itten was a celebrated theorist who
taught at the Bauhaus School of Art, which was
founded in Germany by the architect Walter Gropius
in 1919. The Bauhaus pioneered the principles and
practice of contemporary architecture, art and
interior design. Students were taught radical new
ways to design functional buildings with stark
minimalist interiors. Itten's work included the
development of the concept of 'subjective colours',
which he likened to the colours reflected in the
changing seasons of the year. As he worked with
students, he noticed that each had a natural
inclination to a particular group of colours, and their
personalities seemed to resonate on that group's
special wavelength.

The four seasons

Itten's concept began by splitting colours into two
sections: warm (yellow based) and cool (blue based).
These were then divided again into four harmonizing
groups, which he likened to the four seasons of the
year: Spring/Autumn (warm) and Summer/Winter
(cool). These palettes appeal on a deep, subjective
level and work to support and enhance the
personality of each individual. Each season produces
its own range of colours: spring colours are fresh and
bright; summer colours are soft and light; autumn
colours are deep and muted; and winter colours are
dramatic or icy cool.

Seasonal colour analysis

Johannes Itten's colour theories have been
successfully adapted to colour analysis for choosing
clothes and make-up, but rarely to the choice of
colours for decorating interiors. Yet when his
principles are applied to the home, Itten's concept is
returned to its roots in the Bauhaus, where the
design of architecture and interiors was prioritized.

Colour analysis is generally based on individual
colouring (skin tone, eye and hair colour) and on
personality traits. Everyone is different, and it is rare
for someone to be a 'pure' season. Your 'dominant'
season will be the one that best reflects your
personality. You will find that your dominant
seasonal palette already contains many of your
favourite colours. Other aspects of your colouring
and personality will reveal your 'subordinate' season
of colours. Once you have discovered which seasonal
group of colours fits your personality most closely,
you will be amazed how easily the jigsaw of colour
fits into place and how it can be used to great effect
in the decoration of your home.

These four pictures show how a kitchen can be designed to reflect
each season's individual decorating styles and colour palettes.

1 SPRING This light, airy kitchen uses curved shapes and pale
woods and is decorated in bright, warm blues and creams.

2 SUMMER Traditional kitchen furniture painted in soft white and
then combined with cool yellow and blue-green typifies the
Summer look.

3 AUTUMN Solid, dark wood furniture, old leather and rich spicy
colours are popular with Autumn personalities.

4 WINTER Winter personalities love open spaces, uncluttered
work surfaces and metallic chrome appliances.

Planning colour at home

This book will open your eyes to what can be achieved through the skilful use of colour in the home. No two homes are ever identical, as everyone's taste and personality are different. Even new owners moving into a decorated house will make changes to suit their possessions and lifestyle. Understanding the principles of decorating with seasonal colours and styles reveals your true personality and enables decorating decisions to be made with new confidence and enjoyment.

Once we start to surround ourselves with colours that complement our personalities, choosing colours to create a particular theme or mood becomes quite simple. Our eyes can discern millions of infinitely small differences in colours, and our brains respond to each. For example, blood pressure changes automatically depending on whether we see, literally, red or blue.

Personality and colour

Our personalities instinctively draw us to a particular group of colours and design styles. By understanding the relationship between personality and interior design, we can achieve results that are so sympathetic – so in tune with our personalities – that our home becomes an extension of ourselves and the perfect environment to live and work in.

An understanding of colour can be very useful when design decisions have to be taken by people living together. Conflict can arise when there is a clash of ideas – a clash of seasonal personalities – and compromises are inevitable. Using the seasonal personality and colour theories, it is possible to decorate and live together in peace and harmony.

Colour associations

Many colours conjure up immediate associations. Yellow primarily relates to emotions and practical common sense. Orange often represents sociability, warmth and shelter. Red is perceived as a rich, hot,

Above Clear turquoise walls contrast with white ceiling and woodwork to create a simple, one-colour impact in a hallway.

Right A neutral but warm background allows colourful patterns on furniture, carpet and accessories to act as definite accents.

physical colour. Pink, a paler tone of red, mostly relates to unconditional love and nurturing. Violet is associated with spiritual awareness and blue can be said to govern logic, reason and intellect. Turquoise is recognized as a calm, positive colour. Green represents balance and harmony. We give out certain unconscious messages with the colour of the clothes

we wear, and this, in turn, will influence how we feel or behave. The colours of our environment also enhance these feelings.

Colour and mood

Colour is the primary tool for creating the mood you want in a room. For instance, if you are decorating a living room and want it to stimulate conversation, you may decide an orange colour would be the best choice. The next question is which shade of orange would work best? By studying the seasonal colour palettes, you will find one group that appeals to you above the others.

Autumn personalities, for example, will choose terracotta, rust or dusky peach tones. If you correspond with many of the autumnal personality traits, you have found your seasonal type. By contrast, a Spring person will choose a brighter tangerine orange, and a Summer will not want to use orange at all. The questionnaire on pages 70-71 will enable you to identify your season. Use your seasonal colour palette to identify co-ordinating colours for your decorating schemes, safe in the knowledge that they will always work in harmony with each other.

Choosing the right colours

It is not enough only to select the right colours. It is equally important to choose colours that are appropriate for the use of individual rooms. By studying the language of colour and applying colour theories to interior design, you can create any style and mood. Orange, for example, is a popular colour to stimulate conversation in rooms used for entertaining, but orange walls in a bedroom may inhibit a good night's sleep.

Until recently, there have been many changes in decorating fashions. The bright psychedelic colours of the 1960s gave way to a nostalgic, country-sprigged look in the 1970s. The opulent and exaggerated styles of the 1980s were overturned by

The neutrality of this bedroom's decoration makes a relaxing mood both by day and night. The textures of wood and fabrics are more important here than bright colour.

the simpler way in which we lived in the 1990s, when there was a move towards a more natural style of decoration. In the twenty-first century, the priority is already to create a calm, stress-free environment. The emphasis is on the creation of a home that is in tune with our own individual personality, a goal that can be advanced by the colour theories of this book.

This book will reveal

- How to discover your seasonal colours
- How your personality can influence your choice of home styles and furnishings
- How the seasonal patterns of nature provide insights into the grouping of related colours
- How to plan a specific room from start to finish, taking into consideration individual preferences and lifestyle priorities
- How to select colours inspired by historical and international styles to create interior looks

This bedroom scheme works by introducing bold primary colours against a striking white background. Textures are kept smooth and crisp and accessories to a minimum.

We all need to feel that our home is a safe haven, a sanctuary in which to escape from the pressures of everyday life and, importantly, where we are free to be ourselves. This book is about rooms that really work well for the people who live in them. It is about how to use colour and good decorating ideas to create the perfect home – for you.

1
The Colours

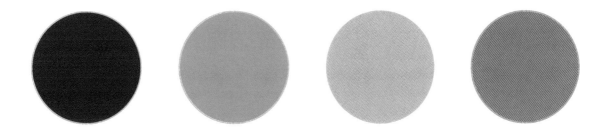

Understanding colour

The universal language of colour sends out messages to everyone who lives in or visits your home

THE COLOUR CYCLE

The colour wheel shows how individual colours can be seen to represent stages in human development and behaviour.

PHYSICAL
survival • passion • motivation

SOCIAL
communication • security • creativity

EMOTIONAL
practicality • confidence • happiness

ENVIRONMENTAL
stability • generosity • harmony

INTELLECTUAL
efficiency • intelligence • calmness

SPIRITUAL
intuition • meditation • idealism

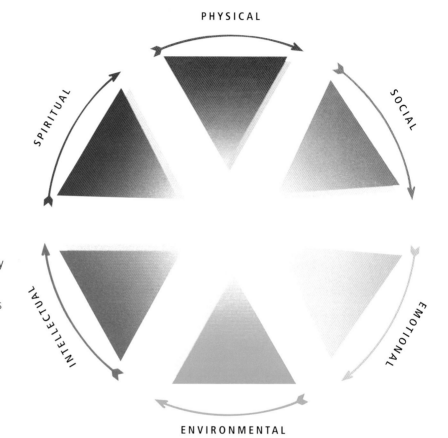

What is colour?

Essentially, colour is light. Everyone has a different perception of colour and objects only acquire colour when light reflects off them or is absorbed by them. In the mid-seventeenth century, the physicist Sir Isaac Newton discovered that when sunlight passes through a triangular glass prism it is refracted into all the colours of the rainbow. He showed that each colour is made up of different wavelengths: red is the longest and the eye has to make large adjustments to see it. This explains why a room painted in dark red appears deceptively smaller than it actually is. At the other extreme, blue and violet have the smallest wavelengths, creating the illusion of distance. Green wavelengths need no eye adjustment at all, which explains why green is perceived as a restful colour and is often used in rooms where a calm atmosphere is required.

The colour wheel

When approaching interior design, it is important to study the effect that different colour combinations will have upon a decorating scheme. In the colour wheel, 'harmonious' colours are those that lie next to each other, whilst 'complementary' colours are found on opposite sides. For peaceful tonal

Spring blues

Summer blues

Autumn blues

Winter blues

decorating schemes, use harmonious colours such as green and yellow or blue and green. Complementary combinations of red and green or blue and orange will create a bright, dramatic effect that is more demanding on the eye.

Basic colours can be lightened or darkened by adding white or black. Lightened colours are called tints and darkened colours are known as shades. The addition of grey to a colour creates a tone of the original. Lighting also affects our colour perception – colours change when seen in artificial or natural light and according to the time of day. For example, blue can look mauve in the evening light.

Finding your favourite blue

These fabric swatches are grouped in toning blues, each swatch representing a different seasonal colour palette. Study each one closely in turn to find out which are your favourite blues – it is these that indicate which season you relate to and which colours you will favour overall. It immediately becomes apparent that very different moods and reactions can be created with different interpretations of the same basic colour. Try to fix the colour of your seasonal blues firmly in your mind so that you can carry out the visual experiment described overleaf.

Discover your personality colour

An understanding of the way colour influences our lives gives us the confidence to create successful interior colour schemes

To feel the potential power of colour and the moods it can create, sit down in a quiet and comfortable place where nothing will disturb your concentration. Close your eyes and relax completely, breathing gently, shutting out the outside world, and imagine a room. Picture yourself, for example, in a totally blue room, the shade of your favourite blue from the fabric samples on page 17. The room can be one in your own home or it can be imaginary. Look around slowly and note whether it is the living room, bedroom or another room in the house. Take in all the detail and then start to observe how you would feel in this room.

If the colour makes you feel happy, relaxed or inspired, take note of your reactions. If the colour makes you feel uncomfortable, open your eyes. A positive reaction tells you this is a colour to use in your home. Negative reactions show that blue is not a colour that you would be happy living with, at least for the present. Although the response to individual colours can be strong, for most people it is rarely entirely negative.

Now move on, choosing a shade of orange, yellow, green, turquoise, purple, red and pink to experience your individual reaction to each colour. Like many people, you may find yourself drawn to warm colours in 'active' rooms, such as kitchens, and to cool colours in 'restful' rooms, such as bedrooms. By objectively observing and recording your response to each colour, you will discover which are your positive colours and the mood they create for you.

Choose your overall favourite colour. This now becomes your personality's 'signature' colour, and you will be naturally drawn to use this extensively in your home. People often discover that this is a colour that they already subconsciously favour for interior decoration and for clothes.

Feeling the impact of colour

Individual colours represent different moods. Instinctively we are drawn to colours with properties that can play an important role in supporting our emotional needs. In addition to discovering your personality colour, you may also find yourself drawn to other colours that you had not previously considered. It could well be that you are going through a period of change or stress, and these colours could give you essential support and energy. Once your circumstances change, you may find these colours less important. Harness this energy and use these colours in your decorating colour schemes with inexpensive accessories such as cushion covers, scented candles, ornaments or fresh flowers.

By looking now at some basic colour theory, we can gain a greater understanding of how to create different moods in various rooms. Studying the link between individual personalities and favourite colours reveals in turn the architectural and design styles we are most likely to be happy to live with. This then gives us the confidence to select the appropriate colours and decorative schemes to help us feel totally in tune with our real selves.

A sunny and welcoming spring yellow in a hallway gives way to neutral shades glimpsed in the living room beyond.

The theory of colour

We are not, of course, the first generation to be interested in the meanings and resonances of colour. Many fascinating colour theories have been developed over the centuries

The exploration of colour

At the beginning of the nineteenth century, the German polymath Johann Goethe evolved a colour wheel and his contemporary Philipp Otto Runge devised a colour sphere. Twenty years later, the French chemist and director of the Gobelins dye-house in Paris, Michel Chevreuil, produced the first definitive colour wheel of graduated shades and tints, work that was continued by Albert Munsell's *Atlas of the Munsell Colour System* in the early twentieth century.

At around the same time, Johannes Itten was one of the first to link colour with personality. His pioneering, intuitive study was partially based on the work of his own students, and linked the colour combinations they chose for their own projects to their personalities. He found that the students produced better work when using colours that they could relate to. Concluding that our personalities lead us to prefer particular shades of a colour, he produced his theory, which centres around what he called 'subjective colour'.

The eminent psychologist Max Luscher developed a colour test that claims to reveal personality traits by the sequence in which colours are chosen. Over the last twenty years, K3 laboratories in London have been working with colour psychology theories. They have adapted Luscher's work and developed a fully computerized Psychological Assessment and Testing System (PCAT) that is used worldwide by psychologists and human resources departments.

More recently, the Scandinavian Colour Institute AG produced the Natural Colour System (NCS). Initially developed in the late 1980s, it was updated in 1995 to include the current system of 1,750 colours. The NCS takes its inspiration from ideas produced by Leonardo da Vinci during the late fifteenth and early sixteenth centuries, and is now widely used as a colour classification system for paints and home furnishings. Theoretically, using the NCS system, it is now possible to classify the full 10 million colours that the naked eye can discern, although to actually do so would be a long process.

Colour choices

There is no one colour that is universally popular. Each one of us prefers the colours and specific shades that are best suited to our personality type. Just as one person may favour contemporary design and another may prefer traditional interior styles, so we are each drawn to the shades of the various colours that most resemble or reflect our own outlook on life. Once we have a basic understanding of our personality colours and how they can be used in interior design, our environment can be planned to support our findings.

The colours
red

The colour of fire and blood, of passion and determination, red provokes strong reactions to its warmth and drama

Physical ▸ survival ▸ passion ▸ motivation

In nature, red warns of danger. On an emotional level, red is associated with passion, friendliness, stimulation and determination. It is a colour which, since the birth of our civilization, has exerted great influence and caused powerful emotional reactions.

Use red with caution in interior design, since a little can go a long way. Reds – deep and inviting – look good in dining rooms, where they impart warmth, but are generally too aggressive to be used in rooms where a calm or relaxed atmosphere is required. Pale Venetian reds look marvellous in sitting rooms and hallways and can take the chill out of cold or north-facing rooms.

Cool reds with bluish or purplish undertones are useful in Summer homes. Spring reds are strong and strident, veering towards the pink. Think mainly of autumn leaves and berries when using reds for an Autumn personality. Scarlet and festive reds, the colour of cranberries, poinsettias and wine, are the favourite colours of Winter personalities, who often accentuate a scheme with a sharp cyclamen pink.

orange

A positive colour, orange represents self-expression, vitality and sensuality, and has the power to lift the spirits

Social ▸ communication ▸ security ▸ creativity

Mixing red and yellow creates orange. It is often perceived purely as a bright children's crayon colour, but in fact tones of orange range from the palest of peaches to the hottest of tropical mangoes. Like yellow, orange is a powerful, warm and stimulating colour that can be used in both historical and contemporary contexts.

Bright orange is effective in corridors, entrance halls and children's playrooms, although it is really too vibrant to be used in rooms that have a more restful or contemplative *raison d'être*. The paler shades of orange, however, can be used in period rooms, and will also lift or update a tired scheme. Again, the oranges derived from earth colours are particularly satisfying for interiors and, when applied with a broken finish, can evoke the warmth and vibrancy of old Italian houses, especially when architectural details are picked out in stone colours in preference to white.

Summer personalities rarely use orange in their decorating schemes. The warm peach and coral tones are popular with Springs and Autumns and work well when used with blues and with greens. Bright, hot orange, however, can be used effectively with strong Winter schemes as a contrast to blue, and even to red.

The colours

yellow

Yellow is the colour of sunshine and of laughter
– it is life-enhancing and stimulates creative and
social activities

Emotion ▸ practicality ▸ confidence ▸ happiness

To many people, yellow represents optimism, creativity and practical
common sense. Pure yellow represents energy and yellow rooms are
nearly always bright and stimulating.

Itten argued that yellow is the colour nearest to pure 'white' light,
which is probably why it works so well and is often seen in rooms that
are used for entertaining. Sitting rooms, living rooms and kitchens are
frequently painted yellow, often with blue as an accent colour. Yellow is
the best colour of all for playrooms, and often the first choice of
children for their bedrooms.

In its wide range of tones from Chinese yellow to palest cream, yellow
is the preferred colour choice of many Spring personalities. Summer
personalities prefer paler yellows, whilst Winter personalities like cool
yellows, essentially white with the smallest addition of a mixture of
pigment. Autumn yellows are at the warmest end of the spectrum and
bring to mind earthy Tuscan ochres.

The colours

green

Green symbolizes new beginnings and prosperity and is the colour that the human eye absorbs most easily

Environmental ▶ stability ▶ generosity ▶ harmony

Green is the colour most closely associated with the world outside, especially during the spring and summer months. It is very much the colour of nature and therefore of the harmony between the natural world and the wider environment.

Situated on the borderline between warm and cool, green works well in almost every interior design context and can be used in all its shades and tones. Dark forest greens look wonderful in living rooms and in libraries, whilst paler greens teamed with pinks and reds can be used effectively in country sitting rooms and bedrooms.

Greens from the Spring palette are clean and crisp, evocative of the colour of new green plants. Soft Summer greens are informal, whilst the darker shades are best used in more sophisticated design schemes. Many Autumn personalities choose green as their favourite colour, whilst a Winter may use pale icy greens as sharp accent colours in a dramatic design scheme.

The colours
turquoise

Thought to have healing qualities, turquoise is favoured by those coping with change and looking towards the future

Medicinal ▶ healing ▶ optimism ▶ transformation

The name turquoise derives from the semi-precious stone first exported from Turkey. It is deemed to have healing properties, and some people also believe it brings good luck. Turquoise is known as a 'universal colour', meaning that it appeals to everyone, and is therefore a popular choice for corporate identities and logos.

As a bridge between the utopian characteristics of blue and the natural harmonies of green, turquoise is a colour ideally suited to bathrooms and children's rooms. Dramatic contemporary living rooms can be created by combining turquoise with deep pinks or corals. The qualities of mental alertness and openness to new ideas, represented by turquoise, make it an inspired choice for the decoration of studies and other workspaces.

Spring turquoises are warm and clear, reflecting aqua tones. Summer turquoises are blue-grey in appearance. Autumn personalities prefer the deep tones that are closer to green than blue; it is the addition of yellow that makes them warm. When turquoise is included in a Winter scheme, it will be to create a peaceful and restful environment.

The colours

blue

The colour of the sky and, by reflection, the sea, blue echoes the infinity of the universe and the depths of the ocean

Intellectual ▸ efficiency ▸ intelligence ▸ calmness

Colour therapists have long recognized that blue is a healing colour and its use is generally believed to assist in intellectual activity, self-expression and cultural pursuits. Soft blues can create a calming and physically relaxing environment for bedrooms, whilst the efficient qualities that blue represents make it a good choice for work spaces.

Decorating with blue can make small spaces look larger: use pale blue in a tiny bedroom and the walls recede. Blue is often perceived as a cold, impersonal colour, but the warm shades found in the Spring and Autumn palettes dispel the myth and can be used to good effect even in dark rooms.

Summer personalities love soft, cool blues, often mixed with small amounts of grey and violet. This is often a colour chosen for bedrooms, where it acts as a calm and serene backdrop to inspirational slumbers. Clear, warm blues, on the other hand, are favoured by Spring personalities, whilst Autumns generally choose blues that are warmed with yellow and which therefore veer towards the green end of the spectrum. Winter blues range from pale icy shades to a dramatic dark blue-black, which is excellent in warm, south-facing rooms, especially those with red accents.

The colours
purple

A colour of mystery and of royalty, purple can be restful and peaceful or grand and imposing, and it provokes a strong response

Spiritual ► idealism ► intuition ► meditation

Purple is essentially a combination of red and blue. The most popular shades, ranging from lilac to lavender, have calming associations. A bowl of lavender in the bedroom or bathroom is relaxing and its perfume is said to help cure headaches and insomnia.

Strong purple can be difficult to use in decoration and normally provokes an equally strong reaction: generally, you either love or hate it! Roman emperors were the first ruling class to use purple for ceremonial robes, and these bright rich shades of purple then became typical of Neo-classical decorating styles in the late eighteenth and nineteenth centuries.

Dark purples tend to be used only in extremely extrovert Winter schemes, but these, or mulberry shades, can make a dramatic alternative to a red dining room. Summer purples include amethyst and shades of plum and can give Summer personalities an elegant but contemporary background to their life. Autumns use reddish-purples, which can be combined effectively with reds and greens. Spring purples are, as you might expect, clear and bright, reflecting shades of violet and lilac.

The colours
pink

Peaceful and soft, pink is an easier colour to use than red, diffusing its heat and strength into something calmer

Sensual ▸ caring ▸ nurturing ▸ romantic

Many pinks are soft and feminine. Our physical response to pink is to produce noradrenaline, which has a peaceful and calming effect. Pink is said to be a supportive colour to people suffering from stress. Pink is flattering to the skin, highlighting its tones.

Pinks range from the slightly sugary pink associated with romance through to the brighter pinks associated with the tropics. As a floral colour, rose pink is a popular choice for bedrooms and bathrooms. Shocking bright pinks, such as cerise and magenta, are best used as accents and for accessories in modern environments. Although pink is often paired with blue, its natural contrast colour is green. The combination of these two colours works well in both traditional and contemporary design.

Warm tones of pink, including shades of salmon and the browny pinks used in period houses, are popular with Autumn personalities. Winters prefer icy pinks or strong magenta, whilst Springs favour clear, warm pinks that work well in living areas of the house and in bedrooms. The cooler summertime pinks are understated and are often combined – like the pinks of sweet peas – with soft blues and gentle yellows.

The neutral colours
brown, beige, cream

The tones of the earth, of the trees and of stone
anchor more extrovert colours and provide a rest
for the eye and the mind

Neutral colours, also referred to as 'natural colours' in the context of contemporary design, are the mysterious agents that permit disparate and often clashing colours to be used together. The spectrum stretches from the varying shades of beiges and creams, through greys, to blacks and whites.

Since they are not true spectral hues (colours of the rainbow), neutrals cannot be said to cause a direct psychological response. We do, however, react subconsciously to neutral colours, mainly through association. They are often perceived as dull, boring colours, but taste has changed towards the use of neutrals as innovative colours for home decoration. The neutral colour palette is effective in softening the dark colours of period interiors, bringing them more in line with contemporary design styles.

Mixing orange with black creates the colour brown. The earth tones of brown are derived from natural pigments found in the soil. Trees, earth and stone all represent the solid, safe qualities we associate with

this colour. At the other end of the spectrum, paler shades of brown range from bamboo to ochre. Hessian, cork and natural woods demonstrate the use of brown in the natural world.

Combining brown with red puts fire and energy into your life and into your interior decorating schemes. Beige browns used with pink create a feeling of nurturing and security. Combined with golden ochre yellows, brown takes on the optimistic qualities of yellow. Brown is most popular with Autumn personalities, with this colour palette reflecting all the shades of autumnal leaves and mellow woods that are their favoured colour territory. Autumns are drawn to natural flooring materials, such as sisal, seagrass and stone.

Beige is a pale version of brown and has no strong sense of identity, working best as a background and accent colour. For a subtle, restful and contemporary decorating scheme, try combining various toning shades of beige and using a single accent of your favourite colour for cushions or accessories. As with any decorating scheme, the secret is tonal balance.

The use of cream softens and warms rooms and is less harsh than white, creating the illusion of warmth, space and light. Made by adding tiny amounts of brown or yellow to white, cream is a colour with safe and reassuring properties. It is the most useful neutral colour in the decorating schemes of Spring and Autumn personalities, who avoid the stark, cooler contrast of pure white.

The neutral colours
black, grey, white

Black darkens other colours and can be oppressive; grey is the most neutral of all; and white contains all the colours of the rainbow

BLACK

Black has long been a popular choice for clothing. It is the colour of protective darkness, but at the same time it can be perceived as being oppressive and overbearing. A combination of black and yellow can remind us of stinging insects, and in Victorian decoration black with mauve – then a new, chemical colour – was popular. Black is used to darken other colours, creating shades of the originals that can give them a brooding intensity.

Unless you are a dramatic Winter personality, black is not a colour you are likely to choose for your decorating schemes. For Winters, black forms the basis of achromatic colour schemes, but works best with coloured accents to lift it and throw it into dramatic relief. A black leather sofa in a striking grey and white room will benefit from some strong magenta or cool turquoise cushions to give visual and emotional interest.

GREY

Grey is the most neutral of all colours. Sober and subdued, grey is not only the colour of bad weather: it also has a brightness of its own when combined with stronger colours. Grey picks up and reflects all the colours around it, particularly if it is used on shiny surfaces such as stainless steel and chrome. Combine grey with another colour and a tone is created. By mixing black and white, different shades of grey can be made, ranging from dark granite and ironstone to the palest dove and silver greys, which are almost white.

Pale grey can be an effective substitute for white in an historic context and is more authentic than a modern beige. Warm grey, sometimes called 'mouse's back', and taupe look stunning over large expanses and are a favourite for carpets designed to expand the space yet provide a neutral background for the other contents of the room.

Mixed with other colours, grey imparts a wonderful misty or smoky feel that is peaceful and evocative. Greys can be particularly useful when you are trying to make small spaces look larger. Applied to a wall in a broken paint effect, grey can bring architectural elegance to the barest of rooms.

WHITE

Although not a spectral hue, white is the most common shade used in decoration and is the agent for creating paler shades from darker colours. White is the symbol of peace – the white flag or the white dove, for example – and in many cultures, brides wear white to symbolize purity. It represents a clean environment and is a popular choice for bathroom fittings, although it can seem stark and unfriendly.

There is more variety to white than just one cold shade. By adding black, grey or cream, you can make many warm and cool shades of white. Whilst the use of white can make a room appear larger, it can also give the illusion of empty and uninviting space. Such a problem can be rectified by the introduction of stronger colours in the furnishings that occupy the central spaces in a room.

True white is used only in Winter decorating, where it highlights dramatic, minimalist, contemporary styles. Summer whites are gentle, and in Summer schemes several tones are often combined to distinguish architectural mouldings and ceilings.

2
Colour in the Home

Planning a room

Successful interior design depends upon careful planning before you embark on a scheme

First of all, take a good look at the areas of the home that you want to decorate. Whatever the size of the project, the principles are the same. Focus on what you already have – furniture and accessories – on your colour priorities and, most importantly, on what you want to achieve. The room information survey opposite will open up the techniques used by professional designers; by using it, you can write your own brief and project specification. Analyse the work involved, define your priorities, list everything you have to do and set a budget. Your notes should include information about the use of the room, combined with ideas and details about walls, floors, furniture, lighting, storage and soft furnishings.

Sources of inspiration
Look around you for inspiration. Take time to imagine your ideal home and how it relates to your current environment. If you have built-in cupboards, for instance, that cannot be moved, a favourite piece of furniture that you cannot live without or soft furnishings that you want to keep and re-use, take these factors into account right from the start. Keep a file of cuttings from magazines or photographs of places you have visited, so that when you decide to decorate you will already have ideas to help you create a supportive environment.

Choosing colours
When planning a decorating scheme, colour is usually the main consideration. Are you starting from scratch or are you updating existing decoration? In either case, think about which colours you'd like to use or bear in mind which colours you already have and want to keep. The simpler your approach to

In this kitchen, the stove is both a focal point and a favourite feature to be retained each time the room is redecorated and updated.

colour, the easier it will be to make decisions about a scheme. Use the natural world as inspiration when planning the distribution of colour in a room. Think of the light sky above and the mid-tones we see around us at eye level, which are then grounded by the dark colours below. The same principles can loosely be applied to decorating schemes. Ceilings should generally be kept pale, if not white; mid-tone colours are the easiest to live with and can be used for walls and furnishings; and the most practical, hard-wearing floor coverings are of mid to dark tones, like the ground beneath our feet.

Finding a focal point

Every room should have a focal point to act as the basis of a colour scheme. This could be a rug, a duvet cover, a picture or an architectural feature, for example, from which colours for the whole room can be drawn. Basic colour schemes should include no more than three principal colours, although additional colours can be introduced as accents if required. Colour is the least expensive way to give a room a new lease of life. Well-worn decoration can quickly and cheaply be updated with accessories in fresh new colours.

Trusting your instincts

The questionnaire on pages 70–71 will enable you to discover your seasonal colour palette and colour personality type. Once you have mastered a few simple rules, you will have the confidence to use the colours you feel happy with and which create your own ideal environment. Feel free to express your own personality and have the courage to mix old and new styles. All advice should be treated as guidelines, not tramlines. If you want to use red in your bedroom in the knowledge that it is energizing and may affect your sleep, the final decision is yours.

Trust your instincts and take the time to try out different patterns and combinations of colours. Remember that colours change according to the time of day. Try painting sample colours on to areas of wall and leaving them there for a couple of days to observe how the colours react in natural and artificial light. Both patterns and colours look different when used over a large area, and it can be useful to get large samples before making any decisions. For example, it may be worth buying half a metre of curtain or upholstery fabric, which can always be used for cushions and accessories.

ROOM INFORMATION SURVEY

Complete this survey for each room of the home and use it in conjunction with the questionnaire 'What season am I?' on pages 70-71.

1 What architectural style is your home?
2 What design styles do you like?
3 What colours do you like?
4 What overall mood do you want to achieve?
5 Which room are you planning to decorate?
6 What are the room dimensions?
7 What are the dimensions of the windows and any other architectural details?
8 Is any structural/building work required?
9 Are there any architectural features you'd like to enhance or improve?
10 What furnishings are required?
11 Who uses the room?
12 What is the room used for?
13 Are you decorating only for yourself or do you share your home with others?
14 Do you and family usually agree on decorating ideas?
15 Is the room naturally light or dark?
16 What time of day is the room mostly used?
17 What is the room's focal point?
18 What can you keep and re-use?
19 What is your budget?
20 What major purchases will be required?
21 What else will be required?
22 Any other considerations?

Proportions and light

Take a close look at your room and consider its proportions and its lighting requirements

PROPORTIONS AND COLOUR

Is the room exactly as you would wish, or are the ceilings too low, for example? Does the room look too dark or too narrow? Skilful use of colour can improve the proportions of any room. Built-in cupboards can also be used to improve the proportions of a room, hiding awkward corners or differences in ceiling levels, for example. It is, in any case, impossible to underestimate the amount of storage space you will need.

Expanding colours

Soft colours that reflect the light can give the illusion of a larger room. Dark colours, on the other hand, can make a large room feel more intimate and can help a high ceiling that may be out of proportion with the rest of the room appear lower. Dark skirting boards can define the shape of a well-proportioned room. Using a pale colour on a low ceiling can, by contrast, make it appear higher and on walls can make a narrow passage seem wider. A long corridor can be made to look shorter by painting the end wall in a darker colour. Use colour to create the effect of architectural moulding. Paintwork can be used to create borders imitating cornices, arches and dado rails. Different tones of the same colour family look very effective when used as wall panels.

LIGHTING AND COLOUR
The quality of light

Successful lighting in a home is achieved by the balanced use of natural and artificial light. Always make the best use of natural light and supplement it with the appropriate type of artificial fittings. Take a

Above The lighting fitted into the risers of these steps is effective yet subtle. It is in keeping with the contemporary style of the area and provides safe passage into the bathroom.

Right Unadorned windows allow maximum daylight into this loft space. This window treatment is only an option if screening is not required for privacy or warmth.

good look at your living space at different times of the day before making any decisions, and bear in mind the times of day when the house is most used. On a practical level, ensure that there are enough power points located in the right places.

Lighting can broadly be divided into five basic types: ambient or overall lighting; functional lighting for specific tasks; accent light to highlight objects; decorative lighting to add atmosphere; and kinetic or moving light, such as candles or firelight. Depending on the uses of a particular room, a number of these types can be incorporated in a lighting scheme. And do not underestimate the power of mirrors: a mirror-wall or large mirror can double the size of a room and reflect colours and decorative details.

Colour influences

Most artificial lights have a colour bias, and it is important to understand the impact this will have on your colour schemes. The colour bias of fluorescent lighting, for example, is ultraviolet and blue, making the surroundings seem cold and distorting warm shades. Incandescent bulbs, on the other hand, give off more red light than daylight and seem yellow. These in turn can distort cool shades.

Ensure you have enough light to accommodate the uses of a particular room. Working and reading, which require concentration and precision, should be undertaken with direct light that does not cast shadows. Full-spectrum light is the closest to daylight. Including dimmer switches where possible is a flexible and inexpensive way to have the facility to create different moods and atmospheres.

Modern lighting can be used in traditional environments, but try to use cream-tone bulbs that cast a softer light. One good rule is to restrict the use of unobtrusive ceiling spotlights to bathrooms, kitchens, halls, stairs and corridors, where there might not be space for additional lighting. Tungsten-halogen lighting is good for contemporary environments, where the sharp white light blends well with streamlined, modern furnishings.

Using the space

Drawing up a scale plan of the room, with everything put in place, is time well invested

A scale plan – most easily drawn on graph paper – is a vital tool to help work out where furniture and fixtures will be placed. It also helps when calculating the quantities of products – such as wallpaper or floor coverings – that you will need.

Storage

Although most people now have an enormous number of possessions, contemporary homes are usually built to be economical with space. As a result, storage has become an important consideration at the early stages of planning a room. Families in particular may need to find space for a very wide range of goods – books, computers, videos and CDs, hobby equipment, toys, tools, as well as the whole range of ordinary household crockery, cutlery, laundry and so on.

Some people like a homely look, but others with a more minimal approach will understand that it is crucial to create streamlined storage. An uncluttered look should be more efficient and can be more relaxing. The good news is that today storage comes in many styles and colours to suit every taste.

Above Neatly stacked CDs are just as effective as decoration on these display shelves as the attractive vases and other ornamental pieces. Tidiness and symmetry are the key to decorative success in this small living space.

Left Many collections of items add clutter to a home, but this assortment of lovely old and worn suitcases and trunks is useful as well as decorative – it functions as a substantial storage system, marked by luggage labels.

Right An unusual clock, carefully hung pictures and an L-shaped seating unit are placed neatly in the corner of this room, but the table on castors and the chair can be moved to give flexibility to the arrangement.

Arranging furniture

Once you have drawn up your basic plan of the room, you can start to position chairs, tables, upholstery, beds and other such moveable items of furniture. One basic rule, which is often overlooked, is to measure up to make sure items of furniture to be brought in can fit through the doors and round and up any staircases!

The arrangement of furniture has to be planned to ensure that doors can be fully opened and people can circulate easily around the room. In the case of

table and chairs, it is important to allow room for the chairs to be moved away from the table without becoming an obstruction. Cupboard doors, for example, need to open up freely without the risk of colliding with other pieces of furniture or architectural elements of the room.

A combination of drawing scale models on your floor plan and physically trying out different layouts on site is the best way to decide upon furniture plans. The time to experiment is before any new purchases are made.

Planning and combining colours

Choosing colours for a room needs a little background knowledge of how they work together

COLOURS AND TONES

Cool colours

The cool side of the colour wheel consists of violets, blues, turquoises and blue-greens. Cool colours are especially effective in small rooms, because they give the illusion of being further away than warm colours and thus make the space seem larger. Warm versions of these colours can be used in north-facing rooms without appearing cold.

Warm colours

The warm side of the colour wheel consists of pinks, reds, oranges, peaches and apricots, yellows and yellow-greens. These create a welcoming mood, and are especially effective in rooms used for entertaining. Warm colours can make imposing, large spaces look smaller and more intimate, and make cold rooms seem less chilly.

Pastel colours

Pastels are the tints of strong colours and are created when white is added to the colours of the spectrum to change the intensity of a particular shade. Decorating with pastel colours is often perceived as being a safe option. However, playing safe can often result in insipid, unsatisfactory schemes in which colour creates little impact. Pastels work best as background base colours, where they make spaces seem larger.

Neutrals

These include the achromatic colours of black, grey and white in addition to brown, beige and cream.

Above Bright, warm colours combine to create a welcoming corner in which to sit and chat. The wide variety of colours used does not seem overpowering because those of the wall and the glasses are repeated in the chair fabric.

Right Neutrals do not have to be boring. Here tonal variety and texture make this space both elegant and cosy. Adding fabrics that are soft and warm, such as fake fur, to interesting rough textures creates an inviting and comfortable mood.

Neutrals are easy to live with and can provide a natural backdrop to colourful furnishings or decorative accessories. Neutrals were often perceived as bland, but today, with natural materials, textures and colours forming the basis of many contemporary design styles, neutrals have come of age. Neutral colours are most effective when they possess interesting textural qualities and are combined with contrasting colours from opposite sides of the colour wheel. Browns and creams inspired by the orange/yellow spectrum contrast well with the grey tones seen in blues and violets.

Tones

A tone is the lightness or darkness of a colour and is portrayed as a descending scale of colour from dark to light, best visualized as the varying shades seen in a black and white photograph. In order to imagine a tone, think of the difference between pastel pink and burgundy red and all the shades in between.

COMBINING COLOURS

Harmonious colours

Taking a look at how nature combines colours will inspire you to create harmonious colour schemes in your home decoration – blue and green, yellow and orange, for example. If you select three or four colours adjacent to each other on the colour wheel, they will always work well together.

Complementary colours

Complementary colours are those on opposite sides of the colour wheel, such as yellow and blue. Complementary colours can be used as contrasts to reduce the effect of a dominant colour. For example, rust oranges can enliven the colours in a predominantly blue scheme. Equal amounts of two complementary colours can be tiring, so it is best to vary their intensity.

Planning patterns and textures

Patterns dictate the theme and mood of a room and textures can work in the same way

PATTERN

Designing a scale

Individual styles use designs in different ways, but always make sure that the use of pattern overall is balanced. Think of patterns of different scales as a family. Use the largest design, the grandparent, on the most dominant surface, such as curtains, where the folds of the fabric will break up the pattern. The mid-scale design, the parent, can be used on a bed or upholstery, and then the smallest patterns, the children, on small areas such as cushions and accessories.

Geometric designs

Often perceived as masculine, geometric designs are now produced in soft, feminine colours. Monotone or two-colour checks and stripes can be informal if used in rustic colour schemes. The classic geometric 'Greek key' design can add a touch of elegant formality to a contemporary room. Small grid designs can serve as textured backgrounds for larger patterns. Winter personalities like sharp, angular designs, Springs love checks and Summers prefer stripes.

Floral designs

Associated with country living, floral designs are now viewed in a new light. Large stylized flowers in bright modern colours can be very effective used in contemporary colour schemes, especially in large airy rooms. Springs and Summers are most likely to include flowers in their decorating schemes, with Springs choosing small prints and Summers larger, more stylized designs.

Above When using monochromatic colour schemes, it is essential to add interest with contrasting textures, such as smooth and rough or loose and tight weaves.

Right The careful use of patterns in this dining room allows the geometric floor tiles to provide a subtle background to the ornate stove and the magnificent clock.

Themed designs

Choosing a particular theme can be a good starting-point when selecting a decorating style, especially in bathrooms and children's rooms. Colour scheming is effortless, as all the colours you need will be present in the patterns. Popular themes include jungle scenes, animal prints and traditional French toile de Jouy landscape and figure prints.

TEXTURE

Mixing soft elements

Combining fabrics, wall-coverings and flooring in different textures can be very effective in colour schemes with little or no pattern. This is an option now made even more accessible by advances in design and production technology. Experiment with the effect of rough, natural materials like brick and

stone in conjunction with smooth granites and silks. Essentially used to create a contemporary look, natural stone, leather and basket-ware can also feature in traditional decorating schemes.

In a room dominated by a single colour, visual interest can be created by the use of a variety of textures. Springs prefer smooth, crisp textures; Summers like soft, silky finishes; and Winters like hard, shiny surfaces. Texture is altogether more important than pattern to Autumns. They are naturally drawn to rough, self-patterned and coarsely woven materials.

Planning floor coverings

Flooring is one of the most important, yet often underrated, elements of interior design. It can also be one of the most expensive and therefore needs careful consideration. The choice of flooring can either link the design schemes of different rooms with one material to give a feeling of space and continuity to a small area, or be used to give each individual area in a larger living space its own identity. Soft colours could be used in the bedroom, water-resistant flooring in the family bathroom and hard-wearing carpet on the stairs.

Depending on the style you have chosen, floors can be left as bare wood or covered with plain or patterned wool carpets. If you are looking for wall-to-wall floor covering, there are the additional options of natural seagrass and sisal floorings. Hard wearing and inexpensive, they are equally effective in traditional or contemporary schemes. Cork and wood can be warm underfoot, whilst stone and marble are cold, but tough in areas of high use.

SURFACES

Wall-to-wall colour

Wall colours and textures dictate the overall feel of a
room, whether warm or cool, large or small, light or
dark, so bear this in mind when selecting paint
colours and finishes.

When planning your colour scheme, the choice of
wall covering should be one of your first decisions.
Today it is possible to create almost any effect with
paper, texture and paint. The wide range of paint
finishes now available means that wall textures can
be anything from matt to glossy. Think about using
stencils to create a pattern that is uniquely painted to
co-ordinate with your colour scheme.

Above The warm yellow chosen for this room is outgoing, sunny
and happy. The ambience would be quite different if, say, cool blue
were used, changing the mood to formal, relaxing and reflective.

Above right Simple blinds are contemporary and informal.
A more ornate treatment here would swamp the small window.

Below right In this open, spacious room of clean, simple lines
one large picture makes more impact than a group of smaller ones
could accomplish.

Choosing window treatments

Windows are the source of light and air into your home. Look beyond fabric curtains and blinds when choosing furnishings for your windows. Painted wooden shutters and blinds can link colours and enhance natural decorating styles.

If your windows look out onto a stunning view, blinds or dress curtains may be all that is needed. When privacy is required, think about wooden shutters or a painted blind that can be decorative as well as functional. If the blinds are to be used all the time, additional thought will have to be given to artificial lighting.

DETAILS

Using accessories

Often neglected and left to the last, accessories can be the key to linking your colour schemes together and completing the look you are trying to achieve. Cushions can balance the colours and patterns used on other surfaces, and artefacts and pictures can enhance your chosen look. Mixing antique and modern pictures and accessories, both expensive items and bargain buys, is a skill worth cultivating. The more eclectic the look, the more individual and less contrived your home will be.

Less is more

One large-scale picture can sometimes be more effective than a collection of smaller frames arranged individually, which create the effect of postage stamps on wide expanses of wall. Small pictures look more disciplined when arranged together to create the illusion of one large picture.

Accessories may not always work in the same room once re-decoration has been carried out. The mood, colours and style may have changed. Don't despair! Before consigning favourite pieces to the attic, look around and see if items can be used in another room or if they can be altered slightly to fit in with the new scheme.

Rooms for all seasons

Each room has priorities to consider when you make decisions about design and colour

Before you start to plan a new decorating scheme, it is important to ask a few questions. Firstly, is the room used for living, working, eating or sleeping? Do you live on your own or are you planning your decorating schemes with a partner? Do you have a growing family to take into consideration?

Secondly, rooms used for different functions have their own sets of rules. Kitchens and bathrooms have to be practical. Small children's rooms have to be designed with safety in mind. Entrance halls and corridors have to be free of clutter to allow movement from room to room. Each room can have an individual style, although in small spaces it can be preferable to link rooms with a common theme. Colour schemes have to be devised to work both in individual rooms and in your home as a whole.

ENTRANCE HALLS

As your front door opens and you, your family or friends walk in, the entrance hall is the first visible room and it will influence the way your home feels and is perceived. A hall is essentially a passageway to get from room to room. Colour apart, make sure you have adequate lighting, especially on staircases, and that the flooring is practical and hard-wearing. Ensure that you have space for hanging coats and ideally a shelf or table for keys and letters.

Signature colours and themes

The entrance hall should set the tone for the rest of your decoration. The colour of the entrance area says a lot about you to your visitors. Neutral tones create a calm atmosphere and allow adjoining rooms to demonstrate their individual styles. Alternatively, the hall and any stairs and corridors can be decorated to

Above If your hall tends to collect clutter, a simple colour scheme has a calming effect. The toning shades used here could be the signature colours for the rest of the house, which would unify the overall effect.

Right Wooden parquet flooring has been laid through a whole area, but the striped rug breaks it up and prevents it from being overpowering. Pale colours on the walls ensure that the space does not become dark and oppressive.

link together the colours used in other rooms. This can be done either by using a patterned wall covering that pulls all the colours together or by choosing a signature colour that is repeated somewhere in every room. Although different rooms can reflect individual looks, there should ideally be a dominant theme that strikes you as you walk in.

Dark colours create a dramatic impact; whereas light colours create a more relaxed and airy atmosphere. If you live alone or without children, pale colours work well, but living with children tokens a different approach and colours that will not emphasize every imperfection.

Seasonal preferences

Spring personalities will want the entrance to their homes to be light, bright and welcoming. Shades of peach, clear yellows and cornflower blues will all be popular choices. The more classic Summers will choose softer, calmer colours like duck-egg blues, sage greens or dusty neutrals. The Autumn hall will be full of clutter and more often than not decorated in strong, rich, spice colours and combined with wooden staircases and natural flooring. The Winter hall will be immaculately tidy, streamlined and, if space permits, coats and hats will be stored out of sight in cupboards.

LIVING ROOMS

Living rooms can have a variety of functions. They can be formal rooms used for entertaining or family rooms that double up as dining and play rooms. Whatever their use, it is important to ensure that living rooms have adequate seating and lighting and that there is room to move around.

Decide what is to be the focus of the room before moving on to colours and themes. If the room has a traditional fireplace, this could influence your style and design; or a large abstract picture could indicate a contemporary tone. Whatever the focal point, it will influence the furniture layout and the activities that can take place in the room.

Colours and styles for living

It is important to select colours that are appropriate for the use of the room. Red is a physical colour and an innovative choice for living rooms used mainly for entertaining, but it will not create a suitable atmosphere if the room is to be used for relaxation and reading. Shades of peach, yellow and neutrals are always a safe bet and can be accented with contrasting tonal colours.

This seating area allows sufficient space for people to move around freely without losing the possibility of intimate conversation. Neutral colours make this a relaxing living room.

Summer personalities will enjoy a more formal living room, possible only used for entertaining, if space permits. Colour schemes are likely to include dusty pinks, blues, lilacs and greens. Summers appreciate a classic fireplace as a focal point and a typical Summer living room might also include a piano. Televisions and sound systems and other obtrusive technology will tend to be concealed in cupboards or under tablecloths.

Large open spaces, which double up as living/dining and possibly kitchen areas, suit Winter personalities. Furnishings will tend to be modern, with achromatic colours schemes teamed with chrome and glass tables, plain blinds and directional lighting. Much of this will also appeal to Springs. Both share a love of light, airy rooms and contemporary styles.

Above Warm colours and large windows to allow in natural daylight make this kitchen an inviting focal point in a family home. Its vivacity helps it to bridge the gap between a functional kitchen and a comfortable living area.

Opposite The emphasis in this kitchen is more on cleanliness and efficiency than conviviality – a style suitable for a serious cook.

An Autumn's living room could have stripped wood floors with oriental rugs, reflecting a preference for natural materials and textures. Large comfortable armchairs and sofas are likely to be covered with woollen throws and an assortment of cushions made from a variety of textures and fabrics. Tables will be strewn with books, magazines and general clutter and little effort will be made to hide things away. All in all, the effect is that of the 'lived-in' sitting room an Autumn feels at home in.

KITCHENS

Kitchens require careful planning to ensure there is adequate provision for storing, preparing, cooking and eating food. For efficient movement around the cooking area, the well-trodden path between fridge, sink and oven should, if at all possible, follow a triangular shape.

The kitchen units dominate the space and will dictate both the room's style and its colour scheme. Much will depend on whether this is a kitchen dedicated to cooking or whether it is also used as an eating and entertaining area.

Colour and style for cooking

Kitchen colour schemes are often based on warm colours. Oranges, peaches and terracottas are said to encourage creativity and yellows are a good choice for bright and stimulating kitchens. Both these colour families look stunning when contrasted with blue. White gives a clean effect and a dramatic look, especially when combined with primary colours.

A Summer's preference for classic styles is evident in the kitchen with the use of traditional units made with laminate doors or painted in the soft dusty colours from the Summer palette. A Spring will choose a bright contemporary look, with fresh and invigorating shades, and a Winter will ensure the kitchen is stark and functional, with stainless steel units probably used as a focal point. An Autumn's kitchen is likely to have dark wood units. The emphasis will be on a natural look: floors may be stone or terracotta; and an Autumn cook may be inspired to decorate the kitchen in the strong colours of spices used in Indian cooking.

Above In a large kitchen, an informal eating area is a bonus. It is especially useful for breakfasts, family lunches or even for casual entertaining of close friends.

Above right Large expanses of doors on storage cupboards can be made more interesting by using pretty trompe-l'oeil effects.

Right This large dining room makes extensive use of red, which serves to bring in the walls and make the space seem cosy, warm and convivial. The informal chairs and the unhung mirror prevent the room from being too imposing.

Far right In an inter-connected sitting /dining room it is best to have a similar style of furniture throughout and at least one linking colour in order to create a unified and tranquil look. The end result is harmonious and spacious.

DINING ROOMS

The majority of contemporary homes now have dining spaces as part of the kitchen area, but summers will love to live in homes that have separate dining rooms in the traditional manner. Traditional hanging lamps and decorative wall fittings will light a room in which a Summer personality will take pride in arranging a formal table for entertaining. An Autumn is unlikely to want a separate dining room. If there is space, the room is likely to double up as a work or hobbies room and have an informal and slightly chaotic atmosphere.

Springs, on the other hand, may well knock through the wall of an existing dining room to make an adjoining kitchen or living room larger, reflecting their openness and sociability. With their love of round shapes, Springs will always choose, where possible, a circular dining table rather than one of a square shape. A Winter will prefer an open-plan space where the look is streamlined, contemporary and uncluttered, decorated in a limited palette of contrasting colours. A glass-top table and a striking modern sculpture in the centre as a dramatic focal point may well be chosen.

BEDROOMS

Generally bedrooms are for sleeping in, but sometimes they are used as an extension of a living room. The bed always dominates, but care must be taken to ensure there is enough storage space. Try to keep bedroom colour schemes restful, in soft colours, to encourage quality rest.

Guest rooms can be a chance to indulge in a more adventurous design scheme, as the room will be used only when friends or relatives come to stay. There is perhaps a colour combination or theme that you have found and liked but were unsure of using in a principal room that could be unleashed here.

Colours for rest and relaxation

Bedrooms should give an aura of comfort and tranquillity in soft and subtle colours. Blues and greens are ideal choices, and a feminine touch is added with pink shades. Bear in mind that strong and dramatic colours are not as restful and yellow,

although stimulating in the early morning, is not a colour that encourages tranquil sleep.

Spring bedrooms will be decorated in fresh, bright colours, combined with crisp, smooth bed linen. Winters will continue their minimalist approach to home decorating with built-in cupboards and simple, modular furniture. Walls are likely to be plain and patterns may be abstract or geometric designs. Summers will create the most restful bedrooms, often decorated in delicate blues or greens, giving a cool, calm atmosphere. An Autumn bedroom may have a traditional brass bed with a patchwork quilt and a mass of cushions.

Above Extravagant use of cushions and the soft drape of fabric behind the bed prevent this black and white guest room from seeming austere. It could double as a reading space by offering the privacy and quiet that are hard to find in a small home.

Right The use of warm colours and soft curtains gives this guest bedroom a warm, light and welcoming feel that is especially important in a north-facing room.

BATHROOMS

Principally functional rooms, bathrooms are dominated by bathtub, shower-unit and associated fittings. A wide variety of innovative colours and styles of sanitary ware is now available. Careful consideration must be given to heating, plumbing, ventilation and storage.

Light to medium blue, turquoise and aqua green shades, all evocative of water, are popular choices for bathroom decoration and are often represented in nautical themes. White is always a safe choice; it can make a small space look larger and co-ordinates with any other colour. If you have a small bathroom, think about using pale, tinted colours as an alternative to white. Mirrors placed above the bath or inside a shower unit can make a room look larger.

Whatever your choice of colours, think of using contrasts from the opposite side of the colour wheel for towels and decorative accessories. If your bathroom has a cold atmosphere, for instance, warm it up with shades of pink, salmon and peach. Bathrooms should be rooms in which you can switch off and relax. Thick, soft towels and aromatic beauty products – combined with candles, soft lighting and plants that flourish in humid conditions – can make these spaces sensuous as well as functional.

Autumns and Summers will choose traditional fittings for their bathing spaces, whilst Winters and Springs are more likely to choose contemporary styles. A Spring will favour a bright, light bathroom. A Winter will be more adventurous, choosing a dramatic contrasting colour scheme, such as black and white with accents of vivid aqua and green.

Left The extravagant bath is the focal point of this room, emphasized by the steps leading up to it. Blue wave patterns in the mosaic wall tiles evoke the sea and piles of luxuriant towels soften the hard lines.

Above White can seem cold and austere in a bathroom. Huge soft towels, panelled doors and bare floorboards combined with flowers and pictures make this a warm and inviting room.

STUDIO LIVING

One-room living presents some interesting colour-scheming challenges. Studios can range from compact bed-sitting rooms to large, converted warehouse loft spaces. Multi-functional styles and colours need to be chosen, bearing in mind that although a studio is essentially one large space, each 'room' area should express an individual mood and style and stand out from the neighbouring space.

Creating rooms within the space

Think of ways to divide the different living zones; screens can be a good option. Windows can be large, making curtains impractical, but fabric hung from suspended poles gives the illusion of curtains and can create privacy in sleeping areas. Free-standing bookcases can divide living and eating spaces and provide good storage. High ceilings also offer the possibility of constructing a gallery that could be used as a separate sleeping or working area. Start by working out what you have to fit into the space, what your priorities are and how much space is required for each area.

Loft spaces usually have high ceilings and a large floor area. Standard pieces of furniture or small pictures can be dwarfed by large open spaces. In smaller bed-sits, multi-functional furniture makes dual use of the space. For example, a raised sleeping platform gives space for a desk or cupboard below.

Below Furniture on castors and lightweight chairs that can be easily moved give flexibility, especially when entertaining. Furniture of different heights, used here on three levels, also helps to define specific areas and activities.

Right Sliding doors provide privacy to bedrooms when required. Blue is a receding colour and gives a feeling of space even when the dividers are closed.

The walls of this boy's bedroom have been colourwashed in blue to last for many years. The style of the easily replaced bedding reflects the current age and interests of the child.

Multi-functional colours

It is sensible to paint all the walls of a multi-functional space in the same colour, basing your scheme around a neutral palette, giving you a 'blank canvas' to play with. Continue the neutral colours when selecting flooring. Rugs are also effective in varying the styles and separating different areas.

The styles and colour palettes preferred by different seasonal personalities can give the same space a totally different look. Springs will love the airy spaces in a loft and could be tempted to recreate the bright pinks, turquoises and greens and modular furniture of the 1950s. Summers are not so likely to enjoy studio living, as they tend to prefer separate, more classic rooms.

Autumns will create a comfortable home, possibly using the best of Indian style. Strong spice colours, Indian artefacts and natural flooring could be combined with rich silk saris used as room dividers. Winters will be tempted either to create a stark modernist interior or, if they live with Autumns, to plan an oriental theme that appeals to both seasons.

CHILDREN'S ROOMS

The main consideration when decorating children's rooms is to use colour schemes and furnishings that can be adapted as they grow up. There is a great temptation to transform a new baby's room with nursery images, but baby themes, especially wallpaper designs, are not going to appeal to a school-age child.

A sensible option is to paint the walls in a plain colour. Neither colours nor patterns should be too strong in the bedrooms of very young children. Pale yellow is a firm favourite with both boys and girls and can be a good choice if you are decorating before the baby is born. Choose simple stripes or checks for curtains or blinds. Keep design themes to duvet covers, cushions and accessories that can be easily and inexpensively changed.

Work, rest and play

Children often have to use their rooms for a variety of activities, although the best colours for each activity are different. Primary colours can be fun and stimulating for young children, and often match their toys. For something different, try combining turquoise with red and green or blue with orange. If a child has difficulty sleeping, confine warm and bright colours and strong patterns to playrooms and use soft colours from the cool side of the colour wheel in the bedroom.

Children should always be involved in choices relating to their own rooms and personal spaces, and it is worth considering their instinctive reactions to colour when decorating their rooms.

WORK SPACES

Working from home has become increasingly common during the last ten years. Design decisions will largely be influenced by where your work space is located and whether it is to be used exclusively as a home office or as a general study area. Home offices can even be fitted under a staircase.

Colours for work

Try to have a colour scheme that you find both inspirational and restful. Yellows are associated with practical minds and oranges with creativity. Deeper shades are best combined with turquoise or blue to avoid over-stimulation. Shades of lilac and mauve are said to aid the thought process and turquoise is the colour to use for clarity of expression. Blue is an excellent choice for work that requires precision and concentration, as it offers an atmosphere of calm and is not distracting.

The seasons at work

Spring personalities will choose work spaces that reflect their happy, bright, innovative approach to life in general. A Summer's office is likely to be understated, tidy and organized, and a separate room rather than an open-plan area if there is the possibility of such dedicated space.

Autumns will often work cheerfully from a desk in a living room, with projects and papers scattered around the room, and will not necessarily choose a separate space. A Winter is interested in anything high-tech and will tend to work from an empty table designed specifically for the purpose, with everything hidden away in cupboards and drawers. A stylish new computer is more likely to be on view than piles of papers and books.

A totally white room with a large window to maximize the daylight makes a practical place in which to create a work area.

GARDEN ROOMS

The conservatory or garden room was first seen in Victorian England, designed to bring the garden indoors during the winter months. Elsewhere, in hotter climates, outside rooms tend to take the form of porches and verandas built to give a place outside to sit shaded from the sun. Traditional conservatories are rarely seen in very hot climates, as even with blinds and fans the glass roofs reflect too much heat.

Above The pink and blue sitting area in this comfortable garden room takes full advantage of the warmth and light. When the darker dining area is lit by candles it becomes a convivial place in which to entertain.

Left This is the spectacular garden room of our dreams: sitting and dining areas are open to the sunshine of the Mexican Pacific coast. Walls are painted in a cool off-white and the sitting area is kept low and simple in design.

Linking the house and garden

Decoration of a garden room can be approached in two ways: as an extension to the room it leads from in the house, with a linked colour scheme; or as a room that brings the garden inside, echoing the colours of the natural world outside.

Of all the seasons, Springs are most likely to want a conservatory, as they are attracted to rooms that allow maximum daylight. They may transform their garden room into a tropical paradise, full of zany colours and exotic pot plants. A Summer will most appreciate a garden room as a shady refuge. The decoration is likely to be traditional, and this room could well be an extension of a living room. A Winter personality will not see a garden room as a priority and Autumns will be inspired to recreate a Tuscan patio with stone walls and terracotta pots.

3
Colour Through the Seasons

Introduction to the seasons

The colours characteristic of each season underpin successful decorating schemes

By observing the patterns in nature, we can learn much about colour harmony. In addition to the colour changes of the seasons of the year, the mood and energy changes at different times of the day – dawn, noon, evening and night.

The colours of the seasons

In temperate climates, spring colours of nature are bright, fresh and warm. During the summer, the look is soft, cool and shaded. In autumn, the colours of the natural world become fiery and mellow. By contrast, winter landscapes are stark and icy cool, and bright colours create dramatic contrasts.

People were once more in touch with the cycles of nature than we are today. For example, before the advent of central heating, the effects of harsh winters effectively ruled people's lives. But if the weather was the cause of hardship and suffering, it also offered the possibility of celebration. Many of the feasts and rituals honoured in pagan and medieval times were associated with the progression of the seasons and the promise of renewal from one year to the next. Now our basic relationship with nature has been largely forgotten.

Some world climates do not exhibit the same seasonal patterns that are found in temperate zones in the northern hemisphere. Johannes Itten's theories of colour are, however, based on such temperate seasons and the energies and colours generated by them. His ideas should be viewed in this context.

Recognizing seasonal colours

All colours are identified by their content of three different elements: a base colour with either warm yellow or cool blue undertones; an intensity of light or dark; and by a clarity, a strength of bright or muted tones.

Different combinations of these three elements form the individual colour palettes of each season:

Spring	Warm; bright, light, clear
Summer	Cool; light, soft, muted
Autumn	Warm; dark, fiery, muted
Winter	Cool; clear, bright, dark

By applying these criteria, you can identify which season a colour relates to; this is particularly helpful when considering home decoration.

Discovering your season and personality type

An increasing number of people now see their home as a supportive environment – an expression and extension of themselves. As a home is nurtured, it can be seen to feed back positive energy to those who live there. By discovering your season and personality type, you will be able to make new connections to your home that will reflect the energy levels found naturally in each season. The description of each season's qualities can be used equally well to describe its unique personality types. Words like energetic, youthful, happy and inspirational all point in the direction of a Spring personality, for example.

Focus on the individual seasonal colours and their distinctive energy levels. Study each of the descriptions of the seasons and different personality types and then complete the questionnaire on pages 70–71. This will help you discover which of the seasonal personalities you identify with most closely.

Using your season and personality type

Once you have discovered your season and personality type, you will find it invaluable when designing your home. Suddenly you will understand why you have decorating preferences and may have found it difficult to live with some styles and colours.

Focus on the section of the book relating to your season. Take inspiration from the styles and colours suggested for your particular personality type. If you share your home with others, study the ideas about living together on pages 74-77 to discover how to create a home that everyone is happy to live in. You may find yourself drawn to looks from another season, or already have these styles in your own home. If you are an Autumn, for example, you may find yourself drawn to Art Deco, essentially a Winter look, but many design themes draw colours and styles from several seasons, and Art Deco is no exception. Winter and Autumn share a love of dark colours and textures and dramatic interiors. In addition to the black and bright colours favoured by Winters, Art Deco interiors can be decorated using strong greens and yellows with bamboo browns

Cool and muted decorating colours and natural plant forms are enlivened here by an intense blue table and a dark curtain that frame the soft look.

from the Autumn colour palette. Focus on the elements that relate to your season and you can create an Autumn Art Deco room.

Many people rush to decorate in the latest home trends. Just as certain clothes fashions do not suit everybody, so the same applies to home decoration. Twenty-first-century design is all about expressing individuality, not being a slave to fashion. Using your seasonal colours and styles, you will instinctively know what is right for you, which in turn will save you from spending money on decoration you cannot live with. You will now be able to approach the design of your home with confidence.

What season am I?

Select one answer from the four choices given for each question

1 Which is your favourite colour?

a   Yellow
b   Blue
c   Green
d   Red

2 Which shapes do you prefer?

a   Round
b   Curves and gentle lines
c   Rectangles with softened corners
d   Triangles

3 Which describes the way you see yourself?

a   Fun-loving, practical, problem-solver who loves new ideas
b   Cool, calm and collected, liking administration and organization
c   Interested in people and in the way things work
d   Unsentimental, self-assured and fascinated by new technology

4 Which accessories do you prefer?

a   Watercolours and artefacts from around the world
b   Silver, china ornaments and impressionistic paintings
c   Natural objects and oil paintings
d   Mirrors, modern art and sculpture

5 Which flowers do you prefer?

a   Flowering pot plants
b   Cut flowers
c   Dried flowers, ferns and twigs
d   Large, single-stem flowers

6 What is your most important consideration when looking for a home?

a   New construction with plenty of natural daylight
b   Traditional and well-proportioned rooms
c   Solid and well-built structure, predominantly rustic in style
d   Spacious, modern, open-plan living areas

7 Which kitchen style do you prefer?

a   Light, airy spaces with pale woods and curved shapes, decorated in bright colours
b   Traditional limed or painted wood, decorated in soft, delicate colours
c   Natural, dark woods and rustic styles, decorated in rich, earthy colours
d   Contemporary, streamlined workspaces with chrome appliances

In the following questions, which words describe the environments you would feel most at home in?

8

a Inexpensive
b Elegant
c Built-to-last
d Hi-tech

9

a Contemporary
b Classic
c Traditional
d Minimalist

10

a Youthful
b Organized
c Comfortable
d Sophisticated

11

a Informal
b Peaceful
c Flamboyant
d Dramatic

12

a Fun
b Graceful
c Individual
d Glamorous

13

a Simple
b Cultured
c Quirky
d Luxurious

14

a Sociable
b Formal
c Welcoming
d Unsentimental

15

a Practical, clean and tidy
b Classic and tasteful
c Environmentally aware
d Modern and stylish

16 Which of the blue fabric samples on page 17 did you select?

a Spring
b Summer
c Autumn
d Winter

17 Look at each season's colour charts on the pages given below; which do you prefer?

a Warm and clear colours (page 82)
b Cool and soft colours (page 98)
c Warm and muted colours (page 114)
d Cool and vivid (page 130)

Add up the number of a, b, c and d responses to the questions and turn to page 164 to discover your season.

Recognizing your season

Use the quick guides here to identify the colours, styles and characteristics of each season

SPRING

Colours	Warm-Bright-Light
Red	Coral red, watermelon, scarlet
Orange	Tangerine, clear peach
Yellow	Sunrise, soft primrose, daffodil
Green	Yellow-greens, clear emerald, jade
Blue	Periwinkle, cornflower, sky blue
Purple	Lilac, damson
Pink	Clear, warm pink, coral
Neutrals	Ivory, pale cream, soft grey, tan, camel

Personality
Sociable, energetic
Flexible, innovative
Practical, problem-solver
Informal, enthusiastic
Helpful and hard-working

Design styles
Provençal
Scandinavian
Retro
Tropical
Mexican

Interior decoration
New, functional houses with natural light
Innovative styles and contemporary furniture
Limed-oak floors, pale carpets and rag rugs
Floral fabrics, checks and stripes
Colourwashed walls; stencils; freehand painting
Light to mid-tone woods – oak, pine, ash
Polished brass, coloured glass, watercolours

SUMMER

Colours	Cool-Light-Soft
Red	Raspberry, cranberry, cherry
Yellow	Pale lemon, grapefruit, buttermilk
Orange	None favoured
Green	Blue-greens, sage, sea-green, dusty jade
Blue	Wedgwood, denim, duck-egg, powder
Purple	Plum, lavender, amethyst
Pink	Rose, orchid, geranium
Neutrals	Soft white, beige, slate, dove grey, pewter

Personality
Cool, calm and gentle
Prefers routine and continuity
Efficient, perfectionist
Classic, traditional, enjoys entertaining
Perceptive and cultured

Design Styles
New English Country
Art Nouveau
Parisian
Mediterranean
Gustavian

Interior decoration
Period houses with architectural details
Classic furniture styles, both antique and modern
Soft carpets, floral rugs, parquet wood and marble
Chintz fabrics, floral designs, co-ordinated colours
Soft, shaded lighting
Mid-tone woods – beech and maple
Antique silver, glass, china, Impressionistic pictures

AUTUMN

Colours	Warm-Deep-Muted
Red	Tomato, burgundy, flame
Orange	Terracotta, dusky peach, cinnamon, rust
Yellow	Gold, ochre, amber, mustard
Green	Olive, lime, moss, forest and chartreuse
Blue	Warm turquoise and aqua, teal, marine
Purple	Aubergine, mahogany
Pink	Soft apricot, salmon pink
Neutrals	Oyster white, cream, bamboo, earth brown, chestnut, slate

Personality

Friendly, loyal and gregarious

Inquisitive and considerate

Extrovert and enthusiastic

Outspoken and sometimes a rebel

Organized and tenacious

Design styles

Shaker

Victorian

Rustic

Indian

Tuscan

Interior decoration

Well-built houses with solid, comfortable furniture

Stained or painted wood, quarry tiles, stone, sisal

Textured linen and raw silk, self-patterned motifs

Antique and decorative paint finishes

Natural ambient lighting and candles

Mid-dark wood tones – mahogany and oak

Antique brass and bronze, oil paintings

WINTER

Colours	Deep-Icy-Vivid
Red	Deep maroon, wine, clear red
Orange	Vivid orange
Yellow	Bright and icy lemons
Green	Emerald, mint, aqua green
Blue	Sapphire, royal blue
Purple	Ceremonial purple
Pink	Magenta, vivid fuchsia
Neutrals	Pure white, black, steel grey, black-brown, charcoal

Personality

Dramatic, with presence

Aspirational, sophisticated

Realistic, pragmatic

Focused, objective

Leader, unsentimental, often ambitious

Design styles

Urban Chic

Art Deco

Classical Revival

Minimalist

Oriental

Interior decoration

Modern, open-plan spaces

Futuristic designs, glass floors and staircases

Shiny surfaces, gloss paint, lacquer, rubber

Geometric or stylized fabrics, plain silks

Directional lighting

Dark woods – mahogany, ebony

Chrome, mirrors and perspex

Living together

When people live together, differences of opinion about decorating often occur

Above Spring and Summer personalities share a bedroom here. Bed drapes and antique furniture add Summer elegance to a fresh Spring look.

Right Spring colours and round shapes co-exist happily alongside the oil painting and comfortable sofa loved by an Autumn personality.

Everyone has quite distinct preferences for colours and styles. Each individual might prefer to spend leisure time in a completely different way, and each may approach a project at work from a different perspective. Those in the fortunate position of choosing a decorative scheme to suit only themselves can select materials by picking only colours which they love and that reflect their own personality. These will create the mood that they feel is most appropriate for their home, and with which they feel perfectly at one.

Finding the common ground

Many people do not live completely alone, and have therefore to consider the views of others. Johannes Itten pointed out that if we are not living with people of the same personality traits and colour preferences as ourselves, we may not be as happy with their selection of styles and colours as we would be with our own.

It is important that everyone feels at ease and happy in their own home. When two people of the same season live together, there is rarely a major conflict of opinion. Life gets interesting when two different seasonal and personality types are sharing a home. Trying to include each individual's preferences in each room by mixing and matching from more than one season will result in an environment that has no coherent mood and ends up pleasing no one.

Decorating a home should be a rewarding and enjoyable experience with a successful outcome. Tensions arise when people fear they are not going to be able to use their own ideas, and the instinctive reaction is to disagree with what someone else has suggested. Does this sound familiar? Tension, and even conflict, can be averted if partners start by asking each other basic questions about their ideas and preferences. Think of yourselves as professional designers – your partner is your client. What are your likes and dislikes? What are your priorities? Look at individual seasons' characteristics together. Common ground can often be found by taking the time to understand another person's characteristics, styles and colour preferences.

The art of compromise

One possible solution to the problem of different seasonal types in the same home is for each family member to choose a favourite room to decorate with their preferred colours. This enables the decoration of each room to be based on a colour palette from one season. People often find they can respond to another season's room if they include a small object or decorative accessory to remind them of their own, so build on this idea.

Influences across the seasons

Compromises can also be made with decisions about texture, form, proportion, shade of colours and use of space. In studying individual looks, you will sometimes see influences from other seasons. Indian styles favoured by Autumns use colours from the Spring palette, for example. Consideration should also be given to existing colour schemes that may have to remain because of budget.

Related colours

Some colours are on the borderline between two seasonal palettes. Study the seasonal palettes of both yourself and other members of your household and you will discover some colours that are closely matched. For example, a Summer maroon is cool and blue based and an Autumn maroon is similar, but with the injection of yellow to make it appear more chestnut in colour. This colour will appeal to both personalities and could be used in a room where a deep red is required.

Linking decorating schemes

Principles and ideas are given to simplify interior design decisions, but it is quirky touches that give a home individuality and character. If common areas of the house are decorated in neutral colours, each room leading off them can breathe. Accent colours can be used to link the decoration from room to room and to reflect each person's favourites. Shades of beige, cream or grey, and of peach, blue or turquoise, are best for unifying colour schemes.

Clockwise from top left

This black and white colour scheme is essentially Winter, but the collection of books and the oil painting add Autumn touches.

The architecture here appeals to Summers; the modernity to Springs; the glass table to Winters; the pots and plants to Autumns.

The soft colours and fabrics and floral bedcovers used in this room will appeal to both Springs and Summers.

Springs will love this light, contemporary room, but Autumns will appreciate the solid coffee table and textured fabrics.

The bright colours of spring

Spring is a new beginning, heralding warmer weather and the renewal of the cycle of nature

In spring, we appreciate the warmer days and notice the arrival of bright, colourful flowers, such as bluebells, daffodils and lilac. Spring and the dawn of each day have striking similarities. Both represent the start of something new, approached with fresh energy and enthusiasm.

Spring moods and colours

The colours of spring that we see in nature are warm, bright and light, with an abundance of yellows, strong clear pinks and lilacs, combined with fresh, spring green leaves. Light – abundant in spring and also the essence of morning – shines through the colours of young foliage and flowers, keeping them pure and luminous.

Spring yellows are pure tones, radiant and clear, representing a spirit of hope, inspiration and happiness. Yellow is often a Spring personality's favourite colour. In Spring decorating, soft, warm creams are used as a natural base colour in place of pure white for ceilings and woodwork. The blues have a hint of red (redolent of the sunrise) to give them warmth. Colours can vary from clear, warm dark blues to soft shades of periwinkle, which, combined with contrasting Spring oranges (ranging from soft peaches to clear colours), can make even a north-facing room feel warm and inviting.

Spring reds are clear and vibrant, with a hint of pink. These shades appeal mostly to people with energetic and vivacious personalities who prefer to live in a home with large windows and plenty of light, one that may well be contemporary in design. The Spring neutral palette harmonizes with the warm

clear colours that this season prefers. They include creams and ivory, caramel, beiges and warm greys – softer shades than pure white.

All spring colours have a yellow base, and nowhere is this more evident than in the fresh, crisp greens that echo those of the young leaves. Practical Spring personalities love garden rooms, especially decorated with shades of green, which act as the link between the house and garden.

The Spring Personality

This list outlines a typical Spring personality, but there is infinite variety within this group. No two people are ever identical.

If you identify with most of the characteristics here, you probably fall into this seasonal category.

▶ Lively, vivacious and effervescent

▶ Warm and outgoing

▶ Informal and relaxed

▶ Impulsive and responsive, with a sense of humour

▶ Highly energetic, sometimes disorganized

▶ Positive and optimistic

▶ Innovative, moves between projects, often leaving them unfinished

▶ Leads by motivating through enthusiasm

▶ Charming, friendly and caring

▶ Values harmony, communicates well, avoids confrontation

▶ Ingenious and imaginative

▶ Quick-thinking and practical

▶ Prefers modern design and a contemporary home

▶ Likes a light, clean and tidy environment

▶ Youthful in appearance and attitude

Top left Spring personalities love natural daylight. The sunlight shining through this vase of tulips and young leaves reflects the luminous, warm colours of spring.

Above Spring rooms are welcoming, sociable and spotlessly clean and tidy. The colours are warm, clear and fresh. The overall look is lively and contemporary.

Left Spring personalities like soft colours, especially when it comes to flooring. Their favourite pictures may be watercolours, with pale wood or soft gilt frames. Springs find round shapes very pleasing. The potted plants and floral prints in this room may reflect a talent for gardening.

The Spring home

Windows in a Spring home are likely to be large and the curtains are likely to be pristine and crisp, often just with simple voiles to let in the maximum light.

Floral favourites

Spring personalities frequently have green fingers. Even if they are not gardeners, they may have potted plants on their window-sills. Springs favour floral fabrics with small motifs, often co-ordinated with gingham checks. No Spring likes harsh geometric lines; Springs prefer curves and round shapes. Tables, china, lamp bases, cushions and decorative accessories will be round or have curved edges. Gathered frills and decorative borders give a feminine quality to Spring homes. Spring personalities are interested in interior design and enjoy decorating. Whereas the other three seasonal types set a high priority on quality, Springs love to pick up a bargain.

Spring interior design styles

Springs are inspired by a wide range of international styles – rustic Provençal; the simplicity of contemporary Scandinavian design; and the bright colours of Mexico and of the tropics. They like their homes to be modern and informal, bright and light.

Mexican and Provençal styles reflect the deepest colour shades of the Spring palette and are particularly suitable for rural living and for the more extrovert Spring personalities. By contrast, the Scandinavian look will appeal to the calmer, more practical side of a Spring personality, and is often well suited to city living.

Seasonal influences

Some Spring design styles are influenced by aspects of the other seasons. A Spring living with an Autumn may choose a Mexican look, because the Autumn partner will love the muted rust and ochre colours and use of natural materials characteristic of the style. A Scandinavian look is essentially an informal

version of Gustavian style, and will therefore find favour with Summer personalities. Both Spring and Summer relate well to the use of soft whites and greens. If a Spring shares a house with a Winter, they will find that Tropical and Retro styles contain common ground. Winters will relate to the use of black in the Retro look and to the bright pinks and generally dramatic colours of Tropical style.

Warm blues and pale wood combine to create a tranquil Spring bedroom and bathroom. Bathed in light during the day, the room never appears dark or cold.

Design Profile

The colours and styles characteristic of spring give clues to the kind of home a Spring personality will want to create.

Overall look
Informal, contemporary

Priority
Light, airy rooms

Colours
Yellow, green, peach and cream

Characteristics
Warm, clear and bright

Patterns
Small floral prints and checks

Textures
Translucent, soft-sheen

Walls
Eggshell, colourwash and stippled finishes

Windows
Big frames, fabric blinds, soft voile curtains

Floors
Limed oak, pale fitted carpet, rag rugs

Furniture
Light woods, modern cane and wicker

Lighting
Natural daylight, bright rooms

Accessories
Brass, coloured and cut glass, watercolours, plants and cut flowers

Spring colour palette

Colours illustrated and numbered below are selected for the palettes
on the 'Creating the Spring look' pages that follow.

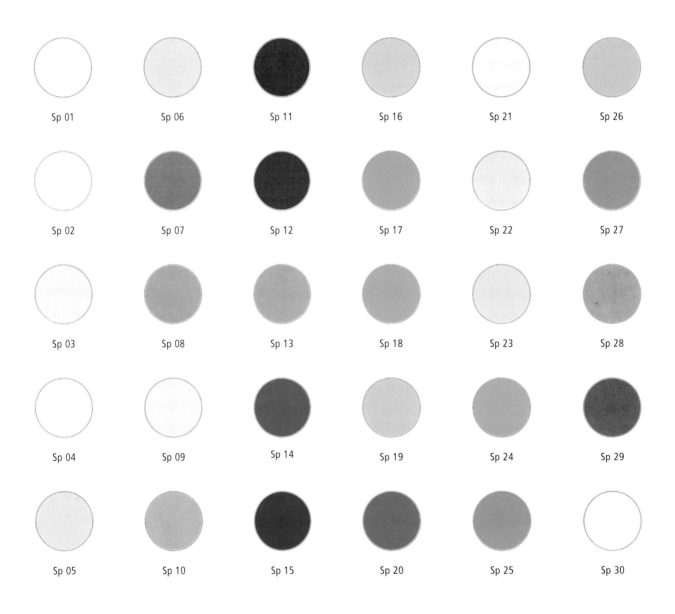

Sp 01	Sp 06	Sp 11	Sp 16	Sp 21	Sp 26
Sp 02	Sp 07	Sp 12	Sp 17	Sp 22	Sp 27
Sp 03	Sp 08	Sp 13	Sp 18	Sp 23	Sp 28
Sp 04	Sp 09	Sp 14	Sp 19	Sp 24	Sp 29
Sp 05	Sp 10	Sp 15	Sp 20	Sp 25	Sp 30

Spring colour combinations

The following is a range of colours for Springs to use. Select a dominant colour to create the desired mood in a room and use it for at least two-thirds of the scheme – the walls, for example.

A secondary, complementary colour is for use over one-third or less of the room to increase visual interest. Other colours can then be used as accents to the scheme, for example, in accessories such as lampshades and cushions.

RED is friendly, welcoming and energetic, adding warmth to a cool room. Turquoise – optimistic yet relaxing – and green – restful and harmonious – are complementary colours. A sense of opulence will be created by combinations of red, purple, turquoise and gold.

ORANGE is creative and sensuous, and gives a feeling of vitality, stimulating conversation and aiding digestion. Blue – calm, relaxed, peaceful and thoughtful – is a complementary colour. Spring dining rooms could combine peach and cream.

YELLOW is spirited, ingenious, imaginative and joyful, providing a feeling of informality and self-confidence. Purple – visionary and powerful – is complementary. A flamboyant mood can be created with Bird of Paradise colours – yellow, red and turquoise.

GREEN is reassuring, harmonious and generous, creating a soothing and refreshing atmosphere. Red – powerful and outgoing – and pink – compassionate and nurturing – are complementary. Nature will be brought into the house with a combination of beige, brown, cream and green.

TURQUOISE is refreshing, healing and optimistic, creating a sociable and positive feel. Red – full of energy and determination – is complementary. To create a sense of wide-open natural space, try green, blue and turquoise.

BLUE is restful, reflective and gentle, giving a cool and peaceful air. Orange – vivacious, enthusiastic and creative – is complementary. Spring work areas could combine yellow, blue and green.

PURPLE is dignified and enigmatic. Yellow – joyful and humorous – is complementary. Peace and tranquillity can be achieved by combining blue, green, turquoise and purple.

PINK is feminine, romantic and sensual, making a room feel supportive and nurturing. Green – soothing and refreshing – is complementary. A feeling of fresh air and freedom can be created by combining yellow, pink, green and purple.

NEUTRALS found in the Spring palette are warm, soft and clear, to harmonize with the other colours in the palette. They include creams and ivories, caramels and warm greys.

Creating the Spring look

provençal

A timeless French style that conjures up images of relaxing holidays and outdoor living

Provençal style reflects a colour palette lit by the bright Mediterranean sun. Provence first became a popular resort in the early twentieth century, when rich families travelled south to escape the cold and damp of winters in northern France.

The style is simple and rustic, characterized by rooms that are very simply and sparsely decorated. Walls are colourwashed in strong earthy colours such as terracotta to complement the texture of the rough natural plaster beneath. Furniture is of carved country wood, usually left unpolished, with rush-seated chairs and fabric squab cushions where some

Above This huge armoir has its door open to reveal that every shelf is laden with the fabric that so typifies the manufacture of the region around Aix-en-Provence.

Left Simple rustic wooden cupboards are a suitable choice for this Provençal kitchen. The brightly coloured flowers in the window bring in a touch of the outdoors.

comfort is needed. Cotton fabrics with small, stylized floral patterns in bright primary blues, reds, greens and yellows on pale cream or white backgrounds are made in the area and are thus characteristic of the style. The fabric may be used for everything from bedspreads to tablecloths and napkins.

The kitchen is the main room of a Provençal house, where the social life of the family takes place. This is a room for eating and for conversation, as well as for the preparation of food. Home-grown produce is stored on open shelves and herbs and lavender gathered from the hills around are hung to dry from hooks in the ceiling beside saucepans and baskets.

Bedrooms are light and airy and often have shutters to keep out the heat, rather than more elaborate window treatments, and rag rugs beside the beds. A patchwork quilt bedcover, in which traditional Provençal fabrics are mixed and matched, would be a fitting accessory for a simple but comfortable bedroom decorated in this style.

The Provençal Palette

Create this look by designing your scheme around the characteristic primary colours. Pale cream or white can be used for base colours and an Autumn terracotta can be introduced for floors and accessories.

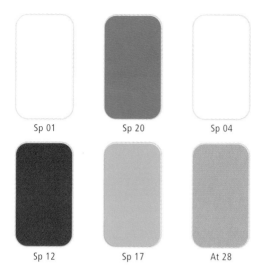

Sp 01   Sp 20   Sp 04

Sp 12   Sp 17   At 28

The Provençal Look

Stone floors

Shuttered windows

Primary colour printed fabrics

Colourwashed walls

Open storage shelves

Dried flowers and herbs

Simple carved furniture

Wrought ironwork

Painted woodwork

Unlined muslin curtains

Rush seats

Above Smooth, hard, light-reflective objects such as marble and glass are cleverly juxtaposed with rough plaster walls and a stone floor.

Left Sun pours through the shutters into this restful dining room, which is enhanced by a cool stone floor and an abundance of untreated wood.

Creating the Spring look
scandinavian

The most sophisticated of Spring styles, combining rustic design and contemporary simplicity

Imagine opening your doors and windows at the end of a cold winter and letting in the fresh new warmth of a Scandinavian spring. The room is uncluttered, with only a few well-designed pieces of furniture. The stripped wooden floors are coloured with paints or with wood stains, or with a chequerboard design in contrasting colours.

The wall decoration of a Scandinavian room is best based on a combination of two or three toning colours. Choose an overall, soft floral design or stencil borders to create a panelled effect. Make the best of the natural light by

Above Panelled walls and integrated cupboards are painted in a solid colour, while lampshade and chair covers are finished with soft frills.

Left Rustic simplicity is the key to this entrance hall. Plain wooden stairs are enhanced by typically Scandinavian carved banisters.

leaving windows bare or by hanging unlined, natural muslin curtains teamed with simple fabric roller blinds. Characteristic Scandinavian fabrics combine simple checks, stripes and single colour floral patterns.

Bedrooms are feminine, with crisp, off-white bed linen, embroidered calico cushions and simple rag rugs beside the bed. Kitchens have open shelves displaying glass storage jars, solid earthenware bowls and pewter accessories.

The Scandinavian Palette

Create this look by using a combination of bright Spring colours and a softer green and deep cream from the Autumn palette. Such a combination will produce the natural tones characteristic of Scandinavia.

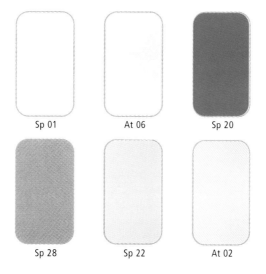

Sp 01   At 06   Sp 20

Sp 28   Sp 22   At 02

The Scandinavian Look

Light and spacious rooms

Natural, toning colours

Bare wooden floors

Tongue-and-groove panelling

Simple painted furniture and floorboards

Unlined muslin or voile curtains

Embroidered cushions

Stencilled designs combined with freehand painting

Single-colour floral, gingham check and stripe designs

Crisp linen decorated with hand-sewn initials and motifs

Plain earthenware and etched glass

Above A detail of the bedroom walls shows the shades of blue used to create the panel effect. The floral design is made with a stencil outline and freehand painting.

Left Toning blues, greens and yellows form the colour scheme of this bedroom. A simple blue and white gingham check is used for the bedspread and blind, with unlined voile for the curtains.

Creating the Spring look

retro

This contemporary look takes its inspiration from the colours and designs of the 1950s

In the years following World War II, everyone was keen to look forward to a new and different future. 1950s style aimed to make good design accessible to everyone through machine production, and was specifically aimed at young people looking to give their first homes an individual, designer look. Today, a revival of the style sees the same designs and colours reproduced to give a bright, stimulating facelift to any room.

The Retro palette of bright contrasting greens, blues and oranges, accented by black and white, in abstract and geometric prints is suitable for living areas. Bedrooms could feature the tiny floral prints that are produced in icy sherbet yellows, aqua blues and aqua greens. Children's rooms can be brought to

life with exciting animal prints co-ordinated with fake fur rugs and cushions. Exotic animal prints can also bring small, dark bathrooms to life.

Modular furniture units, made from Formica if possible, will really set the style. Floors can be covered with natural sisal or geometric lino mosaic – or the look can be recreated with modern vinyls. A room lit with pendant hanging lights and multi-directional wall-lights, ideally with brightly coloured shades, or with slender geometric table lamps, will create the desired atmosphere. A collection of 1950s accessories, such as perspex boxes, melamine or distinctive Poole and Midwinter tablewares, all combine in the recreation of a 1950s home.

Above The strong, clear aqua colour of these kitchen units makes the room a cheerful place to prepare meals. The black and white tiles highlight the red bin and the Formica worktops are typical of the Retro look.

Left Authentic clocks and lamps such as these can still be readily found, and so can modern reproductions, now that the Retro look is back in fashion.

The Retro Palette

Use colour with confidence to create this look. The key word is 'contrast'. Forget about traditional colour matching – large areas of bright colours combine with Winter black to produce fun, funky rooms.

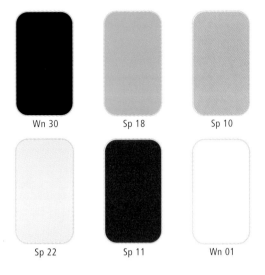

Wn 30   Sp 18   Sp 10

Sp 22   Sp 11   Wn 01

The Retro Look

Young, contemporary and inexpensive

Plain, solid-colour walls

Abstract designs and jungle prints

Strong, bright colours

Contrasting sherbet pastel colours

Stylized small floral patterns

Leather upholstery with metal splayed legs

Modular storage units

Spotlights and uplighters

Melamine, Formica and perspex

Above Black and white floor or wall tiles in a kitchen or bathroom will help create the Retro look, especially when they are combined with strong, bright colours.

Left Strong orange chairs bring an exciting contrast to the black and white chequerboard floor in this predominantly white room.

Creating the Spring look

tropical

The style is informal, full of bright colours that reflect an easy-going and relaxed lifestyle

Tropical style is characterized by simple wooden buildings, often raised off the ground and equipped with verandas and painted shutters. This is a look suited to informal outside living, and can be an innovative theme to choose for garden rooms. Interiors tend to be plain, often with white walls, natural materials and ceiling fans. Choosing unlined muslin curtains, shutters or wood-slat blinds will extend the cooling white theme.

Tropical colours are bright and contemporary, reflecting the brilliance of the flora of these areas of

the world. Walls can be colourwashed in paler tones of the stronger colours. Think of combining rough and smooth textures throughout your decorating scheme. Fabrics include plain linens, stylized leaves printed on simple cotton fabrics, together with batik and tie-dyed textiles.

Tropical rooms are multi-functional and often large and high-ceilinged, so this look naturally lends itself to studios and loft spaces. Furniture is basic and rustic, made from bamboo and rattan. Baskets and decorative accessories of woven palm leaves, stained or left natural, anchor the look. The overall effect is young, naïve and colourful.

Above Inspired by a Caribbean dining room, this space is decorated in soft paint colours of pink, aqua and lilac on pine-boarded walls and simple chairs. The plates and bowls have been produced locally.

Left A Tropical feel is created in a bedroom with simple muslin mosquito nets hanging from bamboo poles. The large leaf motif used behind the bed and the strongly patterned rug give colour and form to the look.

The Tropical Palette

To create this look you need to be adventurous and use vivid turquoises and clashing pinks with the yellows, oranges and lime greens Springs love. Painting the walls white or a pale shade softens the intensity.

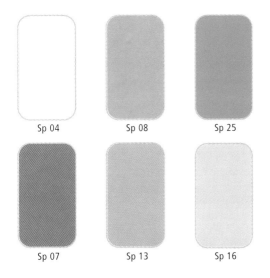

Sp 04   Sp 08   Sp 25

Sp 07   Sp 13   Sp 16

The Tropical Look

Bright tropical colours

Tie-dyed fabrics

Rattan furniture and baskets

Ceiling fans

Colourful paint finishes

Large stylized leaf prints

Unlined muslin curtains and mosquito nets

Hurricane lamps

Hammocks

Rag rugs and runners

Above Strongly coloured flowers and a potted palm may be all that is needed to bring a Tropical touch to a room.

Left In this Balinese room, basic local furniture is piled high with colourful cushions and the large, open space is a cool retreat from the sun.

Creating the Spring look

mexican

Colourful Mexican style is an eclectic blend of Central American and Spanish design

Mexican style as we know it today – bright, abstract and earthy – is a mixture of the designs indigenous to and introduced to the country. Traditional Aztec styles are combined with the Moorish and Catholic patterns and motifs introduced by the Spanish. Typical Mexican houses were basic structures with rough plaster walls and simple woven rugs on natural stone floors. Life centred around the kitchen, often the only substantial room of the house. Every aspect of Mexican design is brightly coloured – particularly the dyed and woven wools – reflecting a long and elaborate history of craft.

Geometric Aztec patterns can be used as the base of a scheme. Mexican colours can be found in the bright Spring palette and are best combined with the mellow Autumn ochres and rusts derived from earth pigments. Rough wall finishes with natural flooring, such as terracotta, stone or sisal, are in order. Blankets can be used as bedcovers, rugs can be used as curtains or tablecloths and ponchos can be hung as decorative wall-hangings.

Kitchen and bathroom schemes easily achieve the full effect of Mexican style by the use of traditional rough earthenware tiles. Freehand borders painted on the walls and on to furniture can echo the designs of the tiles, and decorative accessories of hand-thrown pots and jugs underpin the look.

Above right Pottery and handmade artefacts combined with Mexican woven textiles give a convincing ambience.

Below right Curtains made from typical Mexican weaves are a simple yet dramatic way to create the look, especially if they are combined with a religious picture and a rustic chair.

The Mexican Palette

Find a Mexican rug or throw and base your colour scheme around its colours. Combinations of red and green, terracotta and blue, will create true Mexican palettes – hot, bright and vibrant.

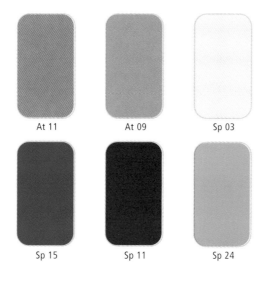

At 11   At 09   Sp 03

Sp 15   Sp 11   Sp 24

The Mexican Look

Natural stone floors

Rough plaster walls

Solid dark-wood furniture

Wooden beamed rooms

Cushions of different sizes piled up as upholstery

Earthenware cookware and pots

Abstract freehand Aztec designs

Multi-coloured rugs

Brightly striped textiles

Throws and ponchos

Above Throws can be used in many rooms, and the extensive use of woven textiles adds a Mexican feel to sofas, chairs and beds.

Left Hand-crafted designs on earthenware pots standing on a stone floor add a touch of Mexico, as does the solid, strongly coloured door.

The soft shades of summer

In the height of summer, cool breezes and shady spaces are really appreciated

During the summer, flowers begin to take on a faded, sometimes burnt-out look that gives a cool grey tone to their colours. The fresh green leaves of spring plants have darkened and taken on a blue-green depth.

Summer moods and colours

Summer colours are cool and soft, and often seem 'greyed' in appearance as a result of their blue undertones. The muted shades are achieved by adding grey to a base colour. Imagine a hot summer's day, when even the sky can look grey, and when the colours are soft through the haze created by the heat.

Blues and greens are key colours in Summer's palette. Blue is often the favourite colour of Summers, representing reliability and a calm, healing atmosphere. Gentle shades of blue will be found in many Summer rooms, especially the bedroom, where it is used to encourage peaceful and deep sleep. For contrasts, it is best to choose soft yellows or pinks, as the Summer palette does not contain any peach or orange shades, which are considered too warm to sit comfortably with the greyed colours.

Summer yellows are cool and soft and work well in situations where colour is being used to make small spaces appear larger. The reds in a Summer palette are quiet and understated, with blue-grey undertones that give the illusion of warmth, even though they are blue-based versions of red.

Visualize a classic English rose, and you will see the Summer shades of pink. As always, the colour is cool and understated, reflecting Summer's gentle, caring

Above This cool green hall is dressed with antique mahogany furniture, and the plaster mouldings and ornaments reflect a taste for the classical.

Above right The Summer who owns this bathroom has ensured that everything is provided for the bathers' comfort, including deep towels and bottles of scented oils. The soft blue wall create a calm, relaxing atmosphere and the style of the bath, pictures and lighting is classical

and even nature. Summer personalities will be drawn to pink almost as strongly as they are to blue. It is almost always seen in their bedrooms and bathrooms, usually combined with a soft blue or yellow as a gentle contrast.

Summer purples include amethyst, mauves and soft plums, similar to those found in the outside world at this time of year. The turquoises of the palette have calming and healing properties. Soft whites and greys form the backbone of Summer's neutral palette. Graded tones of white are often used to pick out and highlight door panels and general architectural features that a Summer personality loves to see in decorating schemes.

The Summer Personality

This list outlines a typical Summer personality, but there is an infinite variety within this group. No two people are ever identical.

If you identify with most of the characteristics here, you probably fall into this seasonal category.

▶ Cool, calm and collected

▶ Quiet, gentle and reserved

▶ Prefers understated, classic design

▶ Likes to work quietly behind the scenes

▶ Perfectionist, nurturing, good listener

▶ Natural diplomat and peacemaker

▶ Perceptive, caring parent

▶ Pays attention to small details

▶ Can appear cool and aloof

▶ Dependable, reassuring and comforting

▶ Well organized and good administrator

▶ Often musical and artistic

▶ Practical, liking routine and continuity

▶ Logical and realistic

Floral wallpaper is the first choice of most Summers for a bedroom. There is a characteristic symmetry in the placement of pictures, lamps and chairs around a chest of drawers.

The Summer home

Summers value peace and harmony, so the atmosphere in their home is likely to be calm, but at the same time ordered and efficiently run. Their strong organizational abilities are put to good use in their homes, and visitors will always find a neat and tidy house.

Classical tastes

Many Summers have classical tastes and evidence of their fondness for music and the arts will often be found in their homes. They may well have a piano, and enjoy painting and embroidery. Classical styles are also evident in their choice of home decoration. Summers like a degree of formality, and will tend to choose furnishings with a touch of elegance. They appreciate antique furniture. The overall look is quiet and restrained.

Summer interior design styles

Well-proportioned rooms and architectural details – such as fireplaces and cornicing – will be priorities. At first glance, Summer homes may seem to be quintessentially English, but this look has translated well into many international styles over the centuries. Traditional Summers will favour the Swedish Gustavian style, where soft, subtle colours are used to paint formal, often antique pieces of furniture. The subtle chic of the Parisian look is right for formal town or country houses anywhere in the world. Summers looking for a more contemporary feel to their home can update the classic English country house style by combining natural seagrass or sisal flooring with traditional chintz. They may opt for a Mediterranean look to create a feeling of timeless and faded elegance.

Seasonal influences

If Summers share homes with Springs, they will both enjoy the modern version of New English Country style and the Gustavian style, or any interiors which combine gentle colours with softly curved shapes

and floral prints. Summers who live with Autumns share a love of subtle tones, high-quality materials and antiques. They may choose to decorate in the Rustic or Shaker styles. The common ground for Summers and Winters living together is spaciousness and order, as well as an attraction to cool colours. The curvaceous lines of the Art Nouveau, Classical Revival or Oriental styles may suit both.

Strong blue reflects the elegance and formality of the furniture in this traditional dining room. The light ceiling and floor and the windows on both sides of the room prevent the room from being too dark during the day.

Design Profile

The colours and styles relating to the summer season give clues to the kind of home a Summer personality will want to create.

Overall look
Classic and elegant

Priority
Good proportions, with architectural details

Colours
Soft whites, cool rose pinks, dusty lilacs, duck-egg blues

Characteristics
Cool, soft and dusty

Patterns
Floral, co-ordinating patterns, figurative scenes

Textures
Chintz, delicate fabrics, silks

Walls
Soft sheens, panels, stippled and dragged paint effects

Windows
Traditional curtain styles, pelmets and trimmings

Floors
Soft wool carpets, floral rugs, parquet wood

Furniture
Classic, formal styles, antiques, polished wood

Lighting
Soft, atmospheric light and traditional table lamps

Accessories
Impressionist paintings, traditional silver, fine porcelain and glass

Summer colour palette

Colours illustrated and numbered below are selected for the palettes on the 'Creating the Summer look' pages that follow.

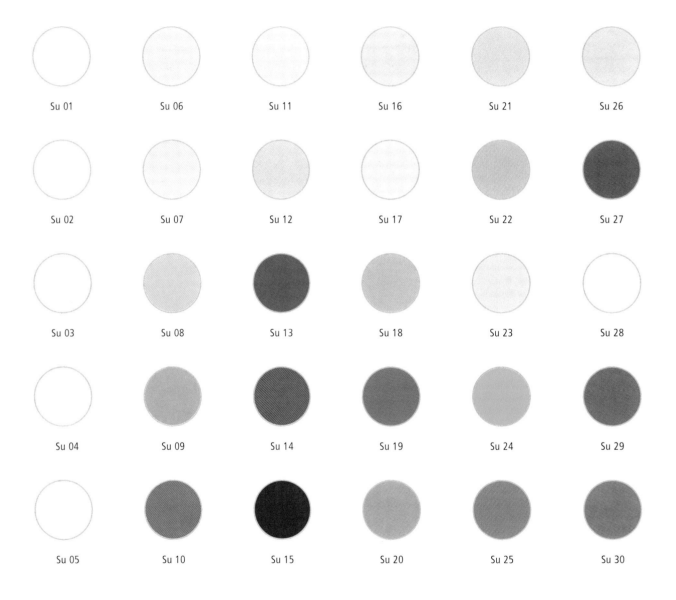

Su 01	Su 06	Su 11	Su 16	Su 21	Su 26
Su 02	Su 07	Su 12	Su 17	Su 22	Su 27
Su 03	Su 08	Su 13	Su 18	Su 23	Su 28
Su 04	Su 09	Su 14	Su 19	Su 24	Su 29
Su 05	Su 10	Su 15	Su 20	Su 25	Su 30

Summer colour combinations

The following is a range of colours for Summers to use. Select a dominant colour to create the desired mood in a room and use it for at least two-thirds of the scheme – for walls, for example.

A secondary, complementary colour is for use over one-third or less of the room to increase visual interest. Other colours can then be used as accents to the scheme, for example, in accessories such as lampshades and cushions.

BLUE is restful, reflective and gentle, giving a cool and peaceful air. Red and yellow – spontaneous and fun – are complementary. Summer work areas could combine yellow, blue and green.

YELLOW is astute, realistic and joyful, providing a feeling of warmth and practicality. Purple – visionary and powerful – is complementary. A flamboyant mood can be created with Bird of Paradise colours – yellow, red and turquoise.

GREEN is reassuring, harmonious and generous, creating a soothing and refreshing atmosphere. Red – powerful and outgoing – and pink – compassionate and nurturing – are complementary. Nature will be brought into the house with a combination of beige, brown and green.

TURQUOISE is refreshing, healing and optimistic, creating a sociable and positive feel. Red – full of energy and determination – is complementary. To create a sense of wide-open natural space, try green, blue and turquoise.

RED is friendly, welcoming and energetic, adding warmth to a cool room and striking in a traditional home. Turquoise – optimistic yet relaxing – and green – restful and harmonious – are complementary colours. A sense of opulence will be created by combinations of red, purple, turquoise and gold.

PURPLE is dignified and dutiful, imparting a mystical atmosphere. Yellow – joyful and humorous – is complementary. Summers love flowers in pink, blue and purple combined with green.

PINK is feminine, romantic and sensual, making a room feel supportive and nurturing. Green – soothing and refreshing – is complementary. Summer dining rooms will be both formal and sensual in berry colours of red, purple and strong pinks such as cranberry and raspberry.

NEUTRALS are soft and cool to harmonize with the other colours in the palette. They include steel greys, soft white, greyed taupe and smoky browns.

Creating the Summer look

new english country

The best of English country house style is updated to something simpler and less formal

Eighteenth-century floral fabrics, the trademark of this style, can be used everywhere. English chintz designs were often based on the flowers found in an English country garden. Combining their colours will ensure colour harmony in your design schemes.

The secret to giving your room a contemporary look is to limit the use of fabric to one basic glazed chintz design, use plain cream cotton for linings and introduce a smaller, co-ordinating sprig design for cushions and accessories. Only use the colours found in your fabric, reflected in contrast bindings on soft furnishings and used as decorative accessories. The cream theme can be extended with a Victorian cotton bedspread as a throw.

Painted wooden panelling, popular in the English Georgian era, can be coloured with toning shades of plain cream and soft beige paint. Continue the paint effects to create original curtain pelmets and update tired pine furniture. Many of the original chintz patterns were derived from Indian embroidery, and this tradition can continue with needlepoint and embroidered cushions as personal and decorative accessories. Natural seagrass flooring and an uncluttered and ordered look will bring this style right up to date.

Above right The floral chintz fabric of bed drapes and curtains is carried through into an en suite bathroom. Extensive use of cream prevents the pattern from being overpowering.

Below right In the bathroom, the matching wallpaper and fabric make a small space appear larger.

The New English Country Palette

This look is based on classic English floral colours, inspired by a country garden in mid-summer. Green is contrasted with pink and blue is combined with green, sometimes with a touch of Spring yellow.

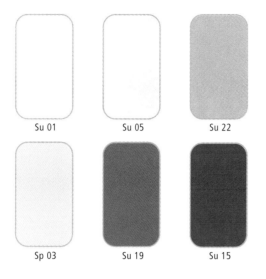

Su 01   Su 05   Su 22

Sp 03   Su 19   Su 15

The New English Country Look

English chintz floral fabrics

Painted wooden pelmets

Simple Georgian-style bed-hangings

Plain painted wall panels

Natural floor coverings

Minimal use of secondary patterned fabrics

Co-ordinated adjoining rooms

Victorian crochet bedspreads

Garden plants and flowers

Simple curtain treatments

Above The piping across the bed-head picks out the strong rose pink of the chintz and the small patterned fabric of the cushions.

Left A bedroom window is well dressed with decorative floral chintz that nevertheless has a light and modern feel.

Creating the Summer look

art nouveau

With its undulating curves, this style was influential at the turn of the 19th and 20th centuries

Art Nouveau – New Art – is an international style with its origins in Britain and Japan, but it takes its name from the French shop, Galeries de l'Art Nouveau, which opened in Paris in 1895. Influenced by nature, the originality of Art Nouveau lies in its ability to take natural shapes and to recreate them in stylized and distinctive motifs.

To create this look, use pale colours such as grey for backgrounds and add the lilacs, greens and yellows that are synonymous with Art Nouveau for soft furnishings and decorative accessories. Take inspiration, too, from the modernist work of the contemporaneous Scottish designer, Charles Rennie Mackintosh, and from the Glasgow School. Keep walls plain, or colourwashed, and combine them with geometric stencil designs to create borders and

decorative panels. Floors should also be left plain, and preferably be made of wood, which can be varnished or stained and covered with a rug.

The Art Nouveau style was used to great effect on both the exteriors and interiors of buildings in America. New Yorker Louis Comfort Tiffany produced coloured glass for windows, screens and door panels and for decorative accessories. His beautiful and elaborate glass lamp shades now seem to typify the romance of this style and are a key factor in creating the Art Nouveau look. Ornaments from the period – including the lithe, stylized figurines – are much sought after and can be very expensive, but many good reproductions are also available. Art Nouveau was, after all, first and foremost, an art of ornamentation.

Above Ornamental wares and sculptures of the Art Nouveau period are very distinctive – they instantly create the look with their sinuous, well-crafted forms.

Left Coloured glass, such as that produced by the American architect and decorator Louis Comfort Tiffany, was widely used for screens, door panels and light shades.

The Art Nouveau Palette

To create this look, combine the softer lilacs, beiges and greens of the Summer palette with Autumn yellows and Winter black. The palette has a striking modernity, consistent with the 'New Art' of the style.

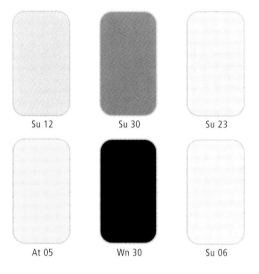

Su 12 Su 30 Su 23

At 05 Wn 30 Su 06

The Art Nouveau Look

Plain off-white walls

Strong naturalistic forms

Light and airy colours

Decorated stained glass

Glass lamp shades

Stylized motifs of flowers, figures, waves

Abundance of ornaments and accessories

Graphic artwork and book illustrations framed as pictures

Wrought ironwork

Above The geometric pattern on the rug is carefully chosen to reflect and repeat that of the chair and light fitting.

Left This room, including the border on the walls and the clock, was designed by the architect and designer Charles Rennie Mackintosh.

Creating the Summer look

parisian

The French chic of high fashion is reflected in elegant Parisian interior decoration

Nothing epitomizes France's love of elegant design more than Parisian interior style. The French are known for only accepting the best in food and fashion, and their approach to decoration is no different. This timeless, controlled, decorative and calm look represents everything Summers love in interior design.

The Parisian colour palette is based around delicate pinks, greens, aquas and blues, accented by off-whites, pale greys and yellows. Pale walls should be

decorated with cornices and intricate architectural details. Aubusson-style rugs on plain polished wooden floors can be a good focal point on which to base your scheme – pick out their subdued and antique colours. Fabrics are used in abundance in Parisian style – for swagged curtain treatments, tented ceilings and wall coverings.

The key to this look is the timeless elegance that would be found in an expensive Parisian apartment. French rooms are formal, highly decorative, but never cluttered. Avoid any modern modular units or harsh spotlights that would detract from the look. Use decorative, classical furniture, which can be combined with inlaid marquetry designs, gilt accents and cut-glass ornaments and lighting. Mirrors and pictures look best in elaborate, gilded frames.

Above The carved and gilded table and the frame of the mirror hung in a central position above it are examples of a classical Parisian style of decoration.

Left This delicate console table, with its plain candlesticks and oil painting, furnishes the hallway of an apartment decorated in classical French taste.

The Parisian Palette

Create the Parisian look by using these soft, toning and sophisticated shades. Keep colour schemes simple. Strong colour schemes can be created with the deeper blues and pinks of the palette.

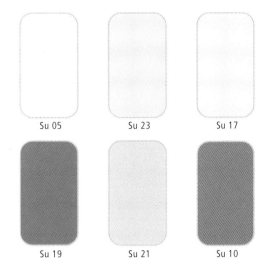

Su 05   Su 23   Su 17

Su 19   Su 21   Su 10

The Parisian Look

Crisp, smart, formal

Silk fabrics

Toile de Jouy fabrics and wall coverings

Tented ceilings

Carved wooden furniture, often gilded or painted

Decorative plasterwork

Chinoiserie ceramics and rugs

Limoges china

Gilded mirrors and picture frames

Above The addition of just a few toile de Jouy cushions will create a Parisian feel, particularly if they are cleverly combined to display several patterns in the same colour.

Left The bedroom is an ideal place in which to use toile de Jouy fabric extensively, because its narrative patterns give a decorative and intimate feel to an interior space.

Creating the Summer look
mediterranean

Colours and designs faded by the light and heat of the sun typify this dreamy style

The Mediterranean landscape has long been an inspiration for painters. To experience the colours of this style, imagine an Impressionist painting where all the dusty shades fade into distant shadows and indistinct outlines. This is the most rustic and informal of all the Summer looks, where the elegance of town design meets the informality of country living. Although the Mediterranean house unites the indoors with the sunny world outside, with doors open to terraces and patios, creature

Above The dreamy colours of this quiet room provide a tranquil retreat from the hot summer sun of a Mediterranean location.

Left Strong daylight brings to life the heavy wooden furniture and floor in this Mediterranean bedroom. The aqua and cream are gentle colours that look good with the dominant warm woods.

comforts are still present in the simplicity. Scrubbed floors combine with crisp linens and romantic lace, and furniture is good and often upholstered.

Mediterranean colours are easy to use because they are all of the same, faded pitch. Create your own combination of blues, yellows and greens, keeping all the tones consistent throughout your colour scheme. The informality of the look comes from plain colourwashed walls and stone or wood floors. Meanwhile, formal accents are achieved with the addition of a few elegant pieces of French provincial furniture.

Mediterranean homes are inspired by the natural world, and this can be reflected in pictures and naturalistic fabric designs. Summers can drape fabrics to create their favourite bed-hangings and curtain treatments, but for this look they should do so without elaborate swags and using unlined fabrics, such as voile.

The Mediterranean Palette

Create this look by using the misty shades of blue, green and yellow, combined with Spring yellow and Autumn peach. Used together, the colours look as though they are seen through a summer heat haze.

Su 18   Su 16   Sp 03

Su 05   Su 22   At 04

The Mediterranean Look

Soft muted colours blended together

Impressionist paintings

Unity between indoor and outdoor spaces

Marble worktops

Window shutters

Natural fabrics, such as linen and lace

Hard surfaces on floors

Country glass and china

Wild flower arrangements

Above An old formal chair against the wall of a living room has a nonchalance that is a disarming element of Mediterranean style.

Left The colours of the floor, walls and faded wooden beams blend together effortlessly, united by their age.

Creating the Summer look

gustavian

This classical Swedish style combines elegant sophistication with country simplicity

Gustavian style developed in northern Europe in the late eighteenth century, and was named after the Swedish monarch, King Gustavus III. It takes inspiration from a mix of French Louis XVI and English Georgian styles, resulting in a harmonious

Above The muslin window drapes in a Gustavian home are simple and unlined, designed to filter and soften a hard northern light.

Left This carved wooden seat is painted in a muted blue-grey and its swab cushion is covered in a typical Swedish check fabric.

and highly decorative look that successfully balances rustic simplicity with elegant sophistication. It is a style that evolved during the following century to become a very attractive decorating option.

The nineteenth-century Swedish painter Carl Larsson depicted an idealized everyday life in his watercolours. His detailed interiors have had a significant influence on the Swedish attitude towards furnishing and decoration, and they remain a good source of inspiration for the rural aspects of the

Gustavian style. Decoration should be kept simple. Woodwork can be painted in soft colours to tone with the colours of painted or papered walls. The main patterns in Gustavian style are used on the walls, either in one or two coloured stripes or in more figurative designs. These patterns can also be used within decorative wall panels.

Fabrics tend to be plain or textured designs, with small checks for cushions and covers. Keep floors uncovered, either painted or stained. Windows can have simple swagged pelmets, perhaps of unlined muslin, which may then be teamed with fabric roller blinds or shutters. The formality and elegance of the look comes from stylized furniture and upholstery, combined with gilt mirrors and frames.

The Gustavian Palette

Create this look by using the cool and understated colours from the Summer palette, together with a darker earth colour from the Spring palette. The coolness of the palette makes clear its northern origins.

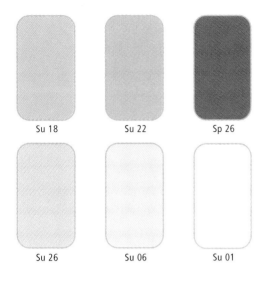

Su 18   Su 22   Sp 26

Su 26   Su 06   Su 01

The Gustavian Look

Natural pale blond wood

Oval gilt frames

Painted borders and panels

Stencilled and freehand designs

Textured stripe and check fabrics

Soft unlined muslin curtains

Chinoiserie designs

Painted and carved wooden furniture

Mirrors and cut glass

Above This detail shows sinuous plant forms in the chinoiserie design of the wallpaper in the bedroom pictured opposite.

Left The heavy frame of the oil painting and the striped wallpaper add formal touches to a room that is otherwise country in style.

The mellow tones of autumn

Autumn offers the vibrant colours of harvest corn, berries and the changing leaves on the trees

Shut your eyes and imagine the distinctive coppers, golds, oranges and rust reds of an American fall and you have the colours of autumn in a nutshell! There is still warmth in the sun before the season passes into crisp, cool, winter days. In autumn there is a mature atmosphere, less frenetic than the energetic vibrations of spring.

Autumn moods and colours

Autumn colours have a strong base of yellow to give them warmth. Adding black can give the illusion of brown. The autumn palette is a multi-faceted mix of mellow tones and bright vibrant colours. If the muted olive, green or beige seem dull, an injection of hot oranges and fiery reds brings them to life.

Orange is the epitome of the autumn spirit. The depth of this colour is reflected in the autumn fruits and leaves that demonstrate the vitality of this season. The colour is a popular choice for Autumn personalities for the living areas of their homes. Its association with food makes it an ideal choice for kitchens and dining areas in particular. The rich and fiery autumn reds can create a welcoming entrance hall, or will encourage stimulating conversation around a dinner table if employed in rooms that are used for entertaining.

Autumn pinks have hints of salmon and peach, warmed with a little yellow. Many of the paler shades of pink will not appeal to an Autumn, who will find them insipid. Yellows are found in many shades and tones in the Autumn palette, ranging from strong clear shades to the warmer ochre and golden mustard yellows. The association with

The yellow-ochre colourwashed walls and warm soft blue door of this Tuscan hall suggest that an Autumn personality is at home here.

spirituality makes the deep, warm autumn purples an inspired choice for rooms for reading and, perhaps, meditation, a pursuit that is likely to interest the Autumn personality.

Autumn turquoises are closer to green than they are to blue and these undertones are echoed in the green palette, which ranges extensively from pale sages to forest greens. Texture is more important to Autumns than pattern, and the neutral Autumn palette therefore displays a multitude of shades. These are used in decorating schemes to enhance textured and self-patterned surfaces, such as fabrics and floor coverings.

The Autumn Personality

This list outlines a typical Autumn personality, but there is an infinite variety within this group.
No two people are ever identical.

If you identify with most of the characteristics here, you probably fall into this seasonal category.

▶ Friendly and gregarious

▶ Insatiable curiosity, interested in the way things work

▶ Good organizer, strong and efficient

▶ Can be unpredicatable, judgemental and bossy

▶ Loyal and an excellent leader

▶ Enthusiastic and innovative

▶ Bases decisions on strong personal values

▶ Can take on too much, but manages to get everything completed

▶ Appreciates quality and durability

▶ Usually loves nature and animals

▶ Sociable, but appreciates solitude

▶ Respects antiquity and history

▶ Energy and enthusiasm come in fits and starts

Above left The red of this comfortable library cum sitting room reminds us of ripe tomatoes, autumn berries and maple leaves.

Left Autumn homes often include greens. Combined with warm browns and beiges, natural textured objects and nature prints, green reflects a love of nature.

The Autumn home

An Autumn home is likely to be full of books and magazines revealing an interest in nature, the environment, engineering and the way people or things work.

Comfortable antiques

Autumns love antique furniture and anything historical, so their homes will be full of family furniture and antique market buys, old books, maps and pictures. Comfort takes priority over style for furniture and the decorating emphasis is on textures.

Autumns are drawn to natural flooring like sisal, seagrass or stone. Rope tie-backs, leather chairs, carved wood, copper pots and traditional lamp bases all have immense appeal. Wood and other materials will be found in abundance – terracotta, brick, pottery, brass and warm-coloured metals – and natural linen and hessian textiles. A large terracotta pot with twisted hazel branches and twigs, placed on a rough, natural stone floor, accents an ideal Autumn home. Sofas and armchairs tend to be oversized, unmatched and often loose-covered. Tables are solidly made in dark woods.

The Autumn colour palette reflects a broad spectrum of colours, and few of the Autumn looks borrow colours from other seasons. Many Autumns have a love of nature and animals. They may live in a city, but their heart tends to be in the countryside. They love open log fires and bringing the natural world inside. Autumns are environmentally conscious and re-cycling will be a priority.

Autumn interior design styles

Neutral colours are often used as the base for Autumn decorating schemes. For a simple and comfortable look with soft subtle colours, the Rustic or Shaker styles are ideal choices. Collectors of antique furniture and ornaments may find a Victorian setting ideal. The bright tones of sari silks that inspire the Indian look will appeal to those Autumns who desire to be adventurous with colour.

Seasonal influences

Autumns and Springs share a love of warm colours and could be equally happy in Scandinavian, Indian or Mexican style homes. Autumns and Summers both prefer period buildings and enjoy Rustic or Shaker styles. Autumns and Winters may find that they have a shared love of Indian style.

The warm colour of the brick fireplace is reflected in the rusts on the comfortable sofa and in the rug. Candles can be lit in the evening to create a cosy atmosphere.

Design Profile

The colours and styles relating to the autumn season give clues to the kind of home an Autumn personality will want to create.

Overall look
Natural, solid and comfortable

Priority
Rooms with a sense of substance

Colours
Creams, golds, greens, ochres, browns and rusts

Characteristics
Natural materials, inspiration from nature

Patterns
Self-patterned designs, Indian or other ethnic prints

Textures
Coarse weaves, velvets, brick and stone

Walls
Antique and decorative paint finishes, rough plaster

Windows
Shutters and blinds, informal curtains

Floors
Wood floors, often stained or painted, sisal and quarry tiles

Furniture
Solid dark wood; large, comfortable, loose-covered sofas and armchairs

Lighting
Natural ambient lighting, table lamps

Accessories
Antique brass and bronze, baskets, ethnic artefacts, oil paintings

Autumn colour palette

Colours illustrated and numbered below are selected for the palettes on the 'Creating the Autumn look' pages that follow.

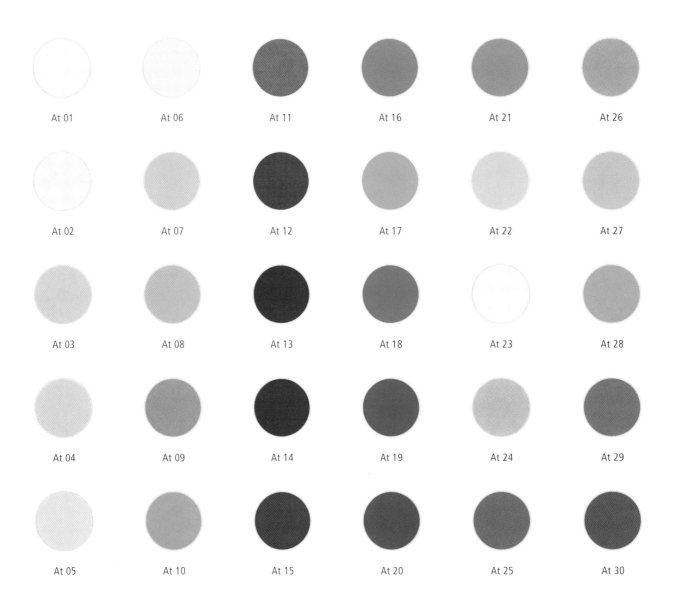

At 01	At 06	At 11	At 16	At 21	At 26
At 02	At 07	At 12	At 17	At 22	At 27
At 03	At 08	At 13	At 18	At 23	At 28
At 04	At 09	At 14	At 19	At 24	At 29
At 05	At 10	At 15	At 20	At 25	At 30

Autumn colour combinations

The following is a range of colours for Autumns to use. Select a dominant colour to create the desired mood in a room and use it for at least two-thirds of the scheme – for example, the walls.

A secondary, complementary colour is for use over one-third or less of the room to increase visual interest. Other colours can then be used as accents to the scheme, for example, in accessories such as lampshades and cushions.

RED is welcoming, intense and energetic, adding warmth and cosiness to a cool room. Turquoise – optimistic yet relaxing – and green – restful and harmonious – are complementary colours. Autumn dining rooms can be fruit and spice colours – yellow, red and orange.

ORANGE is fruitful, passionate and abundant, stimulating conversation and aiding digestion. Blue – calm, traditional, peaceful and thoughtful – is a complementary colour. Autumn leaves and fruits combine burgundy, red, orange and gold.

TURQUOISE is refreshing, healing and optimistic, creating a sociable and positive feel. Red – full of energy and determination – is complementary. A confident and flamboyant mood can be created with Bird of Paradise colours – yellow, red and turquoise.

GREEN is reassuring, harmonious and generous, creating a soothing and refreshing atmosphere. Red – powerful and outgoing – and pink – compassionate and nurturing – are complementary. Nature will be brought into the house with a combination of beige, brown, cream and green.

YELLOW is creative, agile and cheerful, providing a feeling of informality and self-confidence. Purple – visionary and powerful – is complementary. Work areas could combine yellow, blue and green.

BLUE is timeless, reflective and relaxing, giving an efficient and organized air. Orange – vivacious, enthusiastic and creative – is complementary. Peace and tranquillity are achieved by combining blue, green, turquoise and purple.

PURPLE is dignified and enigmatic. Yellow – joyful and humorous – is complementary. A decadent opulence can be created by combining purple, red and gold.

PINK is feminine, romantic and sensual, making a room feel supportive and nurturing. Green – soothing and refreshing – is complementary. A bedroom or bathroom would work well with salmon pink, green and oyster.

NEUTRALS are warm and mellow to harmonize with the other colours in the palette. They include oyster, cream and a range of warm browns and beiges.

Creating the Autumn look

shaker

Pure, simple and uncluttered, this popular style originated in 18th-century America

In the mid-eighteenth century, a group of American pioneers led by an Englishwoman, Mother Ann Lee, set up their own religious settlement in Albany, New York. Known as Shakers, they were a strict Quaker community, who farmed the land for a living and lived in an austere and simple manner. Their interiors were sparsely decorated and furnishings were handmade to a very high standard. Their crafted wooden furniture and cool decorating colours became highly fashionable in the 1980s.

Above The Shaker look is popular for bathrooms, where its functionality and muted paint colours are appropriate and create a simple, contemporary feel.

Left A rag rug added to a room with simple furniture and ladder-back chairs is typical of a style that relies on the thrifty and the handmade.

In today's homes, the Shaker look has a rustic and minimal feel that is wholly contemporary. The colours of the Shaker palette are limited and instantly recognizable, and go a long way towards creating the style. Keep the walls plain and neutral, painted in the less intense shades of the palette. Pattern is created using simple stencil designs, which can also be used on plain wooden floorboards. Floors were made more comfortable by the addition of homemade rag rugs. Woodwork, including skirting boards, panelling and window surrounds, should be painted. Keep windows bare, free of curtains, with shutters or simple fabric roller blinds.

Limit furniture to a few well-chosen pieces of plain wood, perhaps oiled instead of painted, in true Shaker style. Fabrics should be plain or simple gingham check designs. Complete the look with accessories such as hanging shelves displaying pewter mugs, candlesticks or a collection of simple wooden boxes. Storage boxes were a typical Shaker device, used to hide away clutter that might otherwise appear too decorative.

The Shaker Palette

The disciplined colour palette is based on natural pigments, consisting mainly of strong, deep reds, yellows and earth tones, blending effortlessly with warm greens, blues and turquoises.

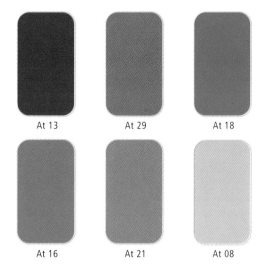

| At 13 | At 29 | At 18 |
| At 16 | At 21 | At 08 |

The Shaker Look

Painted woodwork

Flat, matt-painted walls

Stencils

Patchwork quilts

Ladderback chairs

Pewter cookware, bowls and candlesticks

Wooden hanging pegs

Storage boxes

Rag rugs

Above Shaker households had everything neatly stored away in beautifully sculpted, painted boxes that can be stacked to make an attractive feature.

Left Storage, whether a chest of drawers of basic design or a peg to hang up items such as chairs or the broom shown here, is essential for an uncluttered Shaker look.

Creating the Autumn look

victorian

During the reign of Queen Victoria, the midddle-class home became a symbol of prosperity

Characterized by sombre, dark, cluttered rooms, Victorian design was in stark contrast to the elegant styles of previous eras. Wealth from the new industrial age meant people wanted to show off their new status and affluence, and architecture and interior styles became elaborate and sumptuous.

The Victorian look can be recreated by using dark mahogany, heavy pieces of furniture, richly upholstered seating, ornate rugs, plain or textured velvets and strongly patterned cotton fabrics. Using rich, dark reds and strongly contrasting deep forest greens will instantly conjure up the serious opulence of the Victorian era. Use cornices and decorative mouldings wherever possible. Walls can be divided by a dado rail, with wallpaper above and paint below to give an authentic Victorian feel. This works particularly well in a hallway and stairs.

Carpets and rugs should also be patterned and wooden curtain poles used for window treatments. Curtains or elaborate and weighty fabrics can be designed with heavy pelmets and tie-backs. Trimmings – decorative cording, piping and tassels – are ideal on soft furnishings where possible. Soften the look in bedrooms and bathrooms by using heavy cream lace curtains. Gilt-framed oil paintings and mirrors, large potted ferns and leather-bound books are all perfect accessories for the Victorian look.

Above right The use of rich red, lace curtains and monogrammed towels on an old towel rail adds warmth and luxury to this Victorian bathroom.

Below right This bedroom combines a rich burgundy bedspread with an Arts and Crafts patterned fabric for the bed drapes.

The Victorian Palette

Create this look by using rich, jewel-like colours. Strong crimson reds and deep purples combine with beiges, strong browns, blues and greens. Used together, they create the grand interiors typical of the period.

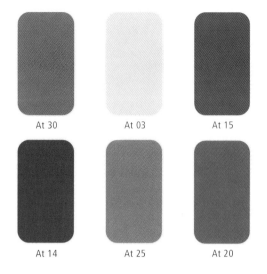

At 30   At 03   At 15

At 14   At 25   At 20

The Victorian Look

Rich, deep colours

Screens

Heavy velvet and brocade fabrics

Trimmings

Dark wood furniture

Lace-trimmed bed linen

Stained glass

Bric-à-brac accessories

Globe lanterns

Brass beds

Above The sumptuous folds of fabric used for the bed drapes in the room opposite are trimmed with cream tassels to voluptuous Victorian effect.

Left An Autumn personality will delight in this book-lined room with velvet drapes and heavy old wood and leather furniture, redolent of the comforts of the Victorian era.

Creating the Autumn look
rustic

The pressures of urban life make us yearn for a simpler way of life, closer to the natural world

Rustic style in the twenty-first century is based on natural materials and simple designs. It goes back beyond the chintz of country style to the stripped-back architecture of real rural life. In doing so, it is paradoxically a very contemporary look. It is an

Solidly built wooden furniture, warm colourwashed walls and exposed beams typify the Rustic look in this simple bedroom.

In this kitchen, colour is mainly provided by the wealth of ceramic jugs, bowls and plates – and the baskets – on the shelves, and by the warm, muted cupboard doors.

informal, eclectic style where there is a noticeable absence of modern materials and technology.

Rustic living centres around the kitchen, which is used for eating, and the living room, where there is always an open fire in a cool climate. The same warm and welcoming effect can be created in hot seasons by using candles in wooden or wrought-iron holders at night. Colourwash the walls in warm colours and use rugs and throws to create a haphazard mix of pattern and texture.

Look for furnishings and furniture made by local craftsmen or old pieces found in local markets. They should be plain, painted or stained and simple in design. Hooks and open shelves can be used for storage, supplemented by baskets and wooden boxes. Tapestry cushions, plain earthenware accessories, such as pitchers and bowls, and baskets of dried herbs and flowers all add a rustic touch.

The Rustic Palette

These colours are inspired by the natural shades of a rural setting. Woodland browns and greens combine with soft oranges and ochre yellow and a periwinkle blue, all from the Autumn palette.

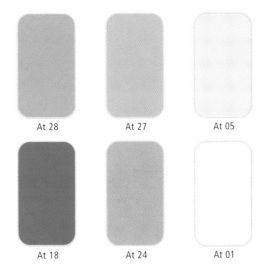

At 28   At 27   At 05

At 18   At 24   At 01

The Rustic Look

Rustic wooden furniture

Woollen throws

Patchwork quilts

Colourwashed walls

Tapestry cushions

Log fires

Country kitchens

Baskets

Earthenware pitchers and bowls

Above The drapes of the bed illustrated opposite are in a neutral undyed fabric, devoid of pattern.

Left Solid, dark-stained floorboards and warm painted walls provide a rustic backdrop to hand-crafted artefacts like the baskets and copper bowls.

Creating the Autumn look

indian

The intricate patterns, cottons and silks and hot spice colours of India give a glow to interiors

Indian printed cottons, woven wools and luxurious embroidered silks have been a part of Western interior decorating styles since the sixteenth century. Such familiar patterns as chintz and paisley originated in India, exported along the trade routes to supply European tastes for the beautiful designs. Their popularity continues to this day.

Using colours with depth and intensity is a key factor in creating an Indian interior. Be bold and use the rich deep shades throughout your colour schemes. The look is eclectic, mixing together textiles and patterns from different regions of the Indian sub-continent. Traditional Mogul hangings, often found with large, flowing floral motifs, can be used as wall decoration, curtains or bed throws. Sari silks, once reserved for dress, now make fashionable sheer curtains and brilliantly coloured cushion covers.

Indian furniture is made from dark woods and is often ornately carved, as are decorative wooden bowls and ornaments. Stylized floral fabrics, hand-printed on to rough cotton, can be used in many ways – as tablecloths, sofa throws, bedspreads and even curtains. Keep lighting levels low and use traditional Indian hanging lanterns made from brass and glass globes. Additional colour can be harnessed by accenting schemes with coloured glass.

Above Red is the dominant colour in this scheme, which gives the room an opulent feel. The various materials work together because of the repeated use of round shapes in their patterns.

Left Richly coloured sari silks draped over the window are a simple yet effective way to introduce an Indian look to a room.

The Indian Palette

Indian colours are inspired by the intense hues of gemstones and by the clear dye tones of sari silks. The brightest shades of the Autumn palette combine with a Spring blue and a clear Winter pink.

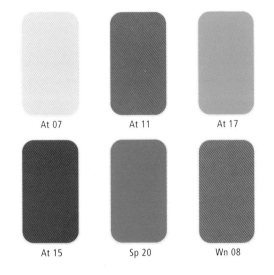

At 07

At 11

At 17

At 15

Sp 20

Wn 08

The Indian Look

Ornate, carved furniture and mirrors

Gilt and brass ornaments

Extensive use of wall mirrors

Mirror glass sewn into fabric

Bright, jewel colours

Silk, cotton and highly patterned fabrics

Fabric used as hangings and bed throws

Candles and incense burners

Above The red, black and gold colours of the wall hanging are echoed in the cushions, preventing the strong colours from becoming overpowering.

Left The walls of this unusual room are richly coloured and strongly patterned and the mirror has an ornate frame – both features that continue a cleverly designed Indian theme.

Creating the Autumn look

tuscan

The terracotta roofs and dusky greens of olive groves in central Italy inspire a gentle look

The rolling landscape of Tuscany, with its horizons punctuated by farmhouses and cypress trees, is the inspiration for this informal, rustic style of strong earth colours. Use terracotta as the base for your scheme, perhaps in a floor of quarry tiles, which can then be complemented by bare plaster walls colourwashed in apricot from the Tuscan palette.

Windows are best left as bare as possible, with any curtains simple and hung from a small metal pole. Light fittings should be rustic in style; wrought iron lamps are very effective. No aspect of the decoration should look contrived.

Create the illusion of stone or marble with paint effects, or paint a mural to imitate a fresco. Rooms are sparsely furnished with simple rustic pieces. Seating areas can be built into the walls with scatter cushions added. Leave brickwork exposed and exploit any architectural features that illustrate the look – such as wooden beams and stone floors.

The Tuscan Palette

Create this look by using rustic colours derived from earth pigments. Shades of terracotta, brown and ochre combine with strong blues and greens that all come from the Autumn palette.

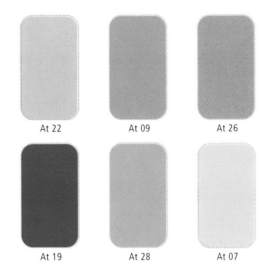

At 22   At 09   At 26

At 19   At 28   At 07

The Tuscan Look

Terracotta floors

Rough plaster walls

Hand-thrown pottery

Stencil decoration

Off-white washed walls

Frescoes

Natural rustic wood furniture

Painted and beamed ceilings

Wrought-iron furniture

Left above The strong, earthy colour of this bathroom draws attention to the rough texture of the plaster walls.

Left below The doors open to the outside and the gentle ochre yellow walls of this dining room give it a simple elegance.

Above Terracotta tiles are the characteristic material used to cover the floors of Tuscan living rooms, and they are now widely available.

Left The natural brickwork, wood mantel and stone floor – and a sunny colourwash on the plaster walls – evoke the earthy colours and textures of Tuscany.

The vivid contrasts of winter

Winter conjures up images of snow and of cold, blue light – vivid and crisp colour tones

Winter colours contrast dramatically: strong deep shades and icy cool tones of a largely primary colour palette throw each other into relief. The night sky is black and intense, the moon appears silver and the stars reflect a cold light.

Winter moods and colours

A cool, blue-based palette reflects a winter climate. Icy pastels, brilliant white and pure black contrast with intense, vivid colours with blue undertones. Winter yellows are acidic lemon; although Winters love strong colours, icy versions of this colour are easier to live with than the deeper tones when used over large areas. These can be kept for use as contrasts and accents. Pale lemons are useful in rooms devoid of natural daylight.

Winters love achromatic schemes. Their favourite spectral hue is red and they do not shy away from using strong shades of the colour. They do not relate to the soft, romantic properties of pink, but they may choose the vivid magentas at the other end of the spectrum.

Purple reflects many of a Winter's personality traits. It is thought of as an assertive, independent colour. The strong, deep tones from the Winter palette enable these vivid cool purples to be used as dominant colours, whereas the other seasons will prefer to use purple as an accent colour.

Winter blues range from icy shades that make spaces appear much larger to almost black-blues, including indigo. This colour is said to put us in touch with our intuition and increase our perceptions. It is an inspiration to writers and

Above An icy pink wall prevents this ultra-modern kitchen from seeming too clinical. The extensive use of see-through materials makes the room seem spacious.

Right This open-plan space is softened by the use of large plants, but most Winters would love to live here, whether plants were included or not.

composers and may induce sleep for those who suffer from insomnia.

The greens in the Winter palette include icy tones through emerald to dark, almost aqua greens with strong blue undertones. The mid-tone versions of this colour are associated with generosity and abundance. If you work from home, it could be beneficial to use the mid-tones of the jade and teal blue-greens in your work space as a restful background to high-tech equipment.

Winter neutrals are the cornerstone of the achromatic colours favoured by Winter personalities. Consisting mainly of black, white and grey, these neutrals will often form a dramatic backdrop to their favourite contemporary design styles.

The Winter Personality

This list outlines a typical Winter personality, but there is an infinite variety within this group. No two people are ever identical.

If you identify with most of the characteristics here, you probably fall into this seasonal category.

- Intense, reliable and ambitious
- Self-assured, stands out in a crowd
- Self-contained; limits friends to a few close ones
- Innovative, often a trend-setter
- Frank, decisive, realizes ambitions
- Detached and objective
- Pragmatic and self-confident
- Respected and admired, can be insensitive
- Realistic, lacks sentimentality
- Natural flair for business and mechanics
- Enjoys administration and organization

The Winter home

Winter homes are like the winter landscape – simple, focused and streamlined – which suits the contemporary Winter design styles well. Preferred surface materials are hard and shiny, such as chrome and glass.

Dramatic contrasts

A Winter's home will be uncluttered and tidy. The basic room decoration is likely to be highlighted by only a few well-placed modern pictures, ornaments or sculptures to provide the focal point in a design scheme, accented by sharp directional lighting.

Design schemes are kept simple, but the colour choices will be dramatic. Black, grey and white are favourites and the colour schemes will often be monochromatic (one colour) or achromatic (having no spectral hues). Any other colour will be an icy pastel or a strong hue such as magenta, blue-toned red, vivid orange or lemon yellow.

Winter interior design styles

Winter interior design styles are contemporary, dramatic and uncluttered, with an influence of classical design. A Winter home is usually a state-of-the-art environment with the latest in lighting schemes, computer equipment and household appliances. A Winter is the only personality type to live in a minimal interior without introducing clutter. Most Winters prefer to live in an urban setting and may choose the Urban Chic look. The simple colours and lines of the Oriental style will also appeal, as will the leather and mirror glass of the Art Deco look.

Seasonal influences

Both Winters and Springs like to live in homes with large windows. Springs want to let in the light, whereas Winters love the feeling of space that windows create. This theme is continued in the use of mirrors and shiny, light-reflective surfaces. Like Autumns, Winters will not make patterned designs their first choice, so fabrics will be plain and furniture

well built and of high quality. They both like silk – pure for Winter and raw for Autumn – and intense colours, so they may find common ground in the Indian look. They also share a love of Art Deco, Shaker and Oriental styles. A Winter sharing a home with a Summer will go for the Classical Revival look.

The stark contrast of a black and white colour scheme is emphasized by a small splash of red. Surfaces are reflective and hard – chrome, glass and plastic.

Design Profile

The colours and styles relating to the winter season give clues to the kind of home a Winter personality will want to create.

Overall look
Dramatic, functional and contemporary

Priority
Rooms with a sense of space

Colours
Bright dramatic primaries, icy cool colours, black

Characteristics
Shiny surfaces, mirrors, contrasting colours

Patterns
Geometric and stylized designs

Textures
Shiny, lacquer finishes, marble, granite, silk and chintz

Walls
High gloss, decorative paint finishes

Windows
Blinds and plain, simple curtain styles

Floors
Dark, shiny wood surfaces, rubber, lino

Furniture
New leather upholstery, metal, chrome and glass

Lighting
Directional lighting, contemporary fittings

Accessories
Mirrors, modern sculpture, posters

Winter colour palette

Colours illustrated and numbered below are selected for the palettes on the 'Creating the Winter look' pages that follow.

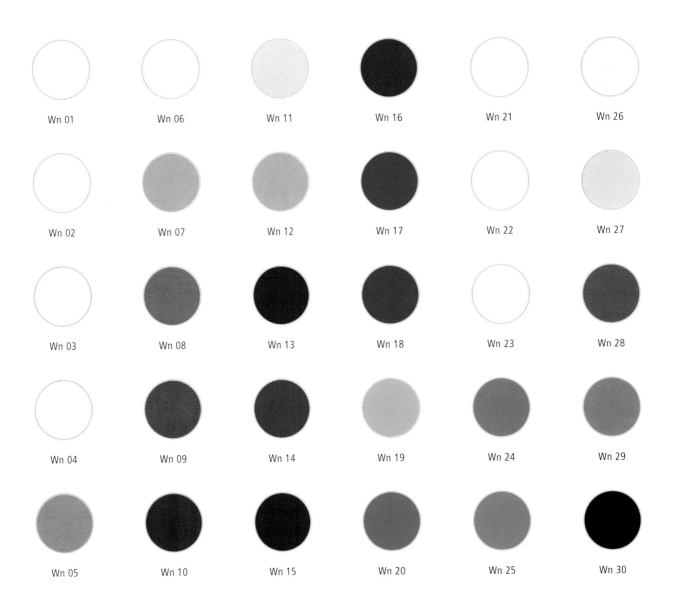

Wn 01	Wn 06	Wn 11	Wn 16	Wn 21	Wn 26
Wn 02	Wn 07	Wn 12	Wn 17	Wn 22	Wn 27
Wn 03	Wn 08	Wn 13	Wn 18	Wn 23	Wn 28
Wn 04	Wn 09	Wn 14	Wn 19	Wn 24	Wn 29
Wn 05	Wn 10	Wn 15	Wn 20	Wn 25	Wn 30

Winter colour combinations

The following is a range of colours for Winters to use. Select a dominant colour to create the desired mood in a room and use it for at least two-thirds of the scheme – for example, the walls.

A secondary, complementary colour is for use over one-third or less of the room to increase visual interest. Other colours can then be used as accents to the scheme, for example, in accessories such as lampshades and cushions.

RED is welcoming, intense and energetic, adding warmth and cosiness to a cool room. Turquoise – optimistic yet relaxing – and green – restful and harmonious – are complementary colours. Recreate winter landscapes with black, white, grey, red and green accents.

ORANGE is fruitful, passionate and abundant, stimulating conversation and aiding digestion. Blue – self-contained, cool and unsentimental – is a complementary colour. Winter dining rooms might add a splash of orange to a simple scheme – black,

white and orange. YELLOW is hearty, frank and decisive, providing a feeling of informality and self-confidence. Purple – visionary and powerful – is complementary. A confident and flamboyant mood can be created with Bird of Paradise colours – yellow, red and turquoise.

GREEN is reassuring, harmonious and generous, creating a soothing and refreshing atmosphere. Red – powerful and ambitious – and pink – compassionate and nurturing – are complementary. Work areas could combine yellow, blue and green.

PURPLE is dignified and enigmatic. Yellow – joyful and humorous – is complementary. A decadent opulence is created by combining red, purple, turquoise and silver.

TURQUOISE is refreshing, healing and optimistic, creating a sociable and positive feel. Red – full of energy and determination – is complementary. Peace and tranquillity will be felt with blue, green, turquoise and purple.

BLUE is timeless, reflective and relaxing, giving an efficient and detached air. Orange – vivacious, enthusiastic and creative – is complementary. A sense of natural open spaces is created with a combination of green, blue and turquoise.

PINK is feminine, romantic and sensual, making a room feel supportive and nurturing. Green – soothing and refreshing – is complementary. A white bedroom or bathroom would be warmed with icy pink, magenta and green.

NEUTRALS are cool, and either very pale or dark to harmonize with the other colours in the palette. They include pure black and white, grey and black-brown.

Creating the Winter look

urban chic

The smooth lines and strong contrasts of this 21st-century style are a fresh approach to city living

Winter personalities love open spaces and their preferred lifestyle includes a home in the city – preferably one that is as modern and smooth-running as possible. The Urban Chic look is streamlined and functional and incorporates an interesting mix of modern industrial materials and eco-friendly, re-cycled products.

Often using the work of young designers, this look concentrates on the maximum exploitation of light and space. Rooms are uncluttered, colours are dramatic and natural materials are often used in conjunction with modern metals. Brick walls and wooden floors stand alongside chrome furniture and

Above Mirrors and reflective metals make the small spaces of modern homes seem larger and brighter – ideal for bathrooms.

Left This kitchen combines classic materials, such as wood, with manmade materials, such as stainless steel. Large mirrors and strong lighting keep the style contemporary.

leather upholstery. Everything is overscaled against a backdrop of neutral colours, with the occasional accent provided by a coloured artefact or work of contemporary art.

The Urban Chic look comes into its own when used to decorate loft apartments and converted industrial spaces in newly populated urban areas, but it can also work well in a barn, mill or other large country space. It is a style for a generous budget, but the end result can be spectacular and durable.

The Urban Chic Palette

Anchored by black and white, this look can be created by adding shades of blue, purple and grey. All are cool and icy, to be warmed up by the complementary use of natural materials such as wood and brick.

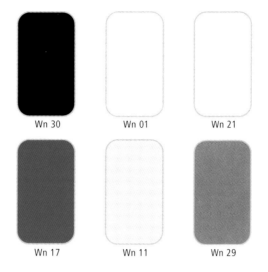

Wn 30   Wn 01   Wn 21

Wn 17   Wn 11   Wn 29

The Urban Chic Look

One-room studio and loft living

Use of industrial materials

Mirrors and mirrored walls

Large abstract paintings

Exposed brickwork

High ceilings

Screens

Metal and glass furniture

Leather upholstery

Dramatic lighting

Above A breakfast bar is given an up-to-date look with a glass top and the industrial appearance of the support.

Left Most of the materials in this room are natural and traditional, yet the use of space and the overall design is essentially modern in feel.

Creating the Winter look

art deco

Cubism, ancient civilizations and
the new machine age all inspired
the geometry of this modern style

In 1925, Paris was the venue for a major design
exhibition – L'Exposition Internationale des Art
Decoratifs et Industriels Modernes – which later gave
its name to the new style of decorative art that
reached its zenith in the 1930s.

Characterized by geometric lines and highly
stylized motifs, Art Deco exploited the possibilities of
mass-market machine production. The inspiration for
its designs was drawn from a wide range of sources
– the abstract forms of the new cubist paintings; the
stepped shapes of Aztec pyramids; stylized figures
from the wall paintings of Egyptian tombs; and the
sleek shapes of new motor cars and ocean-going
liners. It was bright, lively and streamlined.

Sophisticated neutral tones combined with accents
of bold, bright colours typify the look and can be
created with the Art Deco palette. Authentic
furniture from the period is quite easy to find – look
for the distinctive geometric and curved shapes seen
especially in upholstered chairs and sofas and in
decorative mirrors.

Accessories can go a long way towards creating
the look. Geometric wall lamp shades, dramatic
figurines, angular ceramic tea-services, brilliantly
coloured vases, early radio sets, cocktail shakers – all
can still be sourced to create 20s and 30s glamour.

Above A bathroom is an ideal place to use the mirror glass so
typical of the Art Deco style. Wall lights were also extensively used
in designs of the period.

Left The vivid colours used in the stained-glass window help to
light up the neutral scheme of this sitting room.

The Art Deco Palette

This is a vivid colour palette of oranges, greens, purples and black, combined with natural yellows and browns from the Autumn palette. The style spanned Europe and America, using both clear and pastel shades.

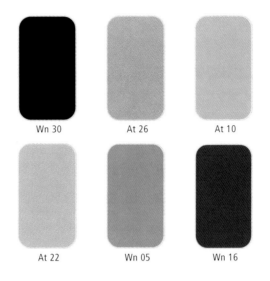

Wn 30   At 26   At 10

At 22   Wn 05   Wn 16

The Art Deco Look

Vivid and pastel colours

Angular and brighly painted ceramics

Leather upholstery

Curved lines

Cuboid shapes

Wall lamp shades and uplighters

Lalique glass

Cocktail cabinets and accoutrements

Mirror glass

Abstract textile designs

Above The Art Deco leather armchair and sofa in this sitting room display a typical geometry in the curved shapes of the arms.

Left Clarice Cliff produced pottery in striking colours and innovative geometric designs in the 1930s. Her ceramics are highly collectable today.

Creating the Winter look

classical revival

Classical styles have been revived at various times and in different ways since antiquity

Winter and Summer share a love of classical design. It is the most traditional of all Winter looks, appealing to this personality because of its dramatic use of colour and uncluttered spaces, but it also encapsulates a Summer's love of elegance. The key

Above A reproduction Roman sculpture on a plinth and Greek bust beside the basin give this bathroom an amusing grandeur.

Above right Dramatic black and white stripes in the bed hangings and valance and a reproduction Greek urn in an elegant Classical Revival bedroom.

to creating this look lies in an easy-going combination of classical elements from earlier revivals – Neo-classicism, Regency and Empire.

The roots of all these revivals are in the architecture and decoration of Ancient Greece and Rome: Neo-classicism was an elegant, symmetrical reaction to the excesses of Rococo; Regency styles concentrated on Greek precedents; and the Empire style gloried in lavish antique forms and draperies. Schemes can be based on black and white, with an injection of natural marble and other stone colours. The addition of gilt and gold Empire furniture and accessories gives drama to an interior.

Keep furniture and accessories to the minimum, so that their elegant forms can be appreciated. Use paint effects to create the illusion of marble surfaces or stone floors. Reproduction statues, perhaps displayed grandly on plinths, give an appearance of of an Ancient Greek or Roman villa in what is, after all, a flamboyant style.

The Classical Revival Palette

Use black and white as base colours, co-ordinated with off-whites and greys and browns from the Summer palette. The look is icy cool, lifted by the addition of gilt and gold on furniture and accessories.

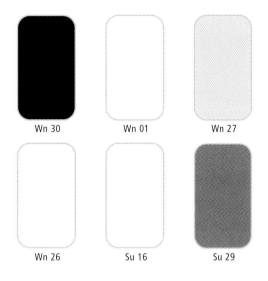

Wn 30	Wn 01	Wn 27
Wn 26	Su 16	Su 29

The Classical Revival Look

White walls

Gilt frames

Decorative mouldings

Gilded curtain poles

Tented ceilings

Draped curtains

Rich textures

Formal carved furniture

Alcoves and plasterwork

Tassels and trimmings

Above Black and gold, together with white, are key colours in a Classical Revival palette. This room uses a formal patterned wallpaper to effortlessly create the effect.

Left The fireplace, alcoves and moulded architraves of the painted ceiling in this living room are essentially classical in style.

Creating the Winter look
minimalist

The ultimate in contemporary, streamlined living, this style does away with any hint of clutter

Minimalist design takes its first inspiration from the Modern Movement and the diverse work of its many designers throughout Europe during the twentieth century. Hot on the heels of the Hi-Tech innovations of the 1970s that celebrated industrial production, Minimalist interiors first appeared during the 1980s.

The style developed into a cool aesthetic that celebrated open spaces, geometric shapes and the total absence of pattern. Rooms were stripped of any unnecessary ornamentation and design schemes were often built up around a focal point of one large picture, object or piece of furniture. Base your scheme on just two colours, with solid blocks of

contrasting colours as accents. Low-voltage lighting is ideal, with dedicated pools of directed light to create dramatic effects.

Surfaces should be kept bare, with everything stored in cupboards – preferably with plain doors designed to look like part of the walls. The illusion of pattern can be created by the use of different textures on surfaces and with one-colour textiles with tactile weaves and pile.

Above The contemporary materials of woodblock floor and metal chair work well in a room with one bright colour introduced for the orange wall.

Left Low geometric furniture is typical of the style, giving the illusion of wide horizontal spaces.

The Minimalist Palette

White is the key colour to create the Minimalist look, used in conjunction with black and grey. An injection of one strong bright colour – purple, orange or yellow – is used for dramatic and vivid contrast.

Wn 30	Wn 13	Wn 05
Wn 21	Wn 01	Wn 03

The Minimalist Look

Bare rooms

Solid colours

Plain walls

Painted/natural wood floors

Plain, geometric furniture

Mix of textures

Metal furniture and light fittings

Dramatic pictures and accessories

Strong, directional lighting

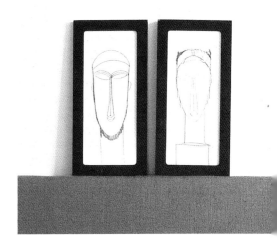

Above Two small black and white etchings in simple black frames placed symmetrically over the bed are the only adornment to the white walls.

Left Crisp, white bed linen reflects the white of the walls and continues the neat simple lines of this Minimalist bedroom.

Creating the Winter look

oriental

East meets West in a style that
blends and balances elements
from both cultures

Oriental homes are functional and very disciplined
in design. Furnishings are simple, often based around
a neutral colour scheme of natural beiges and
creams, accented with black and the stronger colours
found in decorative lacquerware and ceramics. The
mix of traditional styles from the Orient can be
reinterpreted to create an ideal contemporary style.

Walls and floors should be plain. White or cream
walls with natural wooden floors are ideal, with
seagrass mats. Use traditional Shoji screens in place
of cupboard doors or as innovative room dividers.
Windows are kept bare, with shutters or Venetian
blinds in place of curtains. Oriental homes have low-
level furniture: bamboo chairs, simple, armless
upholstery and futon beds all work well.

The Oriental Palette

The rich lacquer reds and strong blues that are synonymous with Oriental style work well with neutral shades and with strongly contrasting black and white. The colours are clear, sharp and clean.

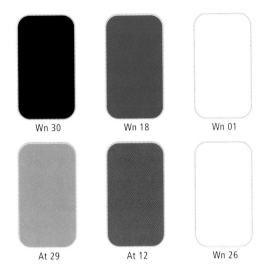

Wn 30   Wn 18   Wn 01

At 29   At 12   Wn 26

The Oriental Look

Natural woods

Futon beds

Shoji screens

Low-level furniture

Lacquerware

Figurative imagery

Calligraphy

Seagrass mats

Paper lanterns

Sunken baths

Above The rituals associated with bathing are important considerations in Japanese homes.

Above left Paper lanterns behind a black lacquer side table, together with silk cushions and Oriental calligraphy on a slender hanging, characterize the style.

Left The paper screens in this dining room are uniquely Oriental. Ornamentation is simple and kept to a minimum, ensuring that black lacquer chairs and table retain a sharp silhouette.

Above A bust from the Far East, especially if it is of a spiritual nature, brings an Oriental feel to any room. Here, it is juxtaposed with a collection of red lacquerware that continues the style.

4
Historical Inspirations

Introduction

Historical interior design forms and colours can supply ideas for contemporary schemes

Above The decorators of Pompeii adorned interior walls with brightly painted mythological and domestic scenes.

Right Classical proportions are seen here in perfectly balanced architecture and idealized human figures.

An informed look at the history of architecture and interior colour can be an inspiration for the styles of decoration we use in our homes today. Colour has influenced interior design since our ancestors first painted the walls of caves, and each culture and era has produced its own individual palette. In earlier centuries, the choice of colours was limited to those derived from the natural pigments available, but expanded as new chemical dyes were invented. An enormous range of hues is on offer today.

As styles evolved, ideas were often borrowed from the work of previous generations of decorators. In England, for example, the Victorians revived the colours and forms of Gothic architecture, and the Edwardians were strongly influenced by the colours and Neo-classicism of the Georgian era. Many contemporary styles are also inspired by the past, or adapt their characteristics within a modern scheme. For example, a period room with original architectural mouldings painted in plain and subtle colours can form a stunning backdrop for bright contemporary furnishings.

CREATING A HISTORICAL STYLE

There are many reasons why you may decide to create an entire reproduction of a period look. You may want to enhance the existing architecture of your home or you may want to give depth of character to a modern environment. It is well worth spending time researching the elements of your chosen style, particularly its colours and furnishings, although you can be flexible in your interpretation. Design has always developed gradually and has always been adapted to suit different climates, cultures and tastes.

EARLY ORIGINS

An interest in the design of interiors can be traced back to the great ancient civilizations. The Ancient Egyptians were master painters with strong red, yellow, green and blue pigments derived from plants and minerals; and brightly coloured murals and decorative paint panels, dating from the first century AD Tang period, have been found in China.

The Ancient Greeks and Romans devised principles of architectural proportion that have served as a benchmark for designers ever since. Derived from the forms and measurements found in nature, these classical proportions have a harmony that seems so correct that they have been revived and re-used consistently over the centuries.

The following pages provide brief but apposite glimpses into the overall styles and, particularly, the colour palettes used to enhance interiors in the West from the Middle Ages through to this century. The ideas of the past documented here may influence our own ideas for the future.

Early styles of decoration in Europe

MEDIEVAL ▶

Early medieval houses throughout Europe were simple, timber-framed, one-room dwellings built around a central fire. By the thirteenth century, the fireplace tended to be placed against a wall and some simple wooden furniture – tables, chairs and storage chests – was introduced. Walls of grander houses were painted with floral, geometric or heraldic motifs, often in greens and golds. By the fourteenth century, tapestries and linen, wool and silk fabrics in rich pigment dyes of white, blue, green, russet, violet and scarlet were used as hangings and as wall, table and bed coverings.

TUDOR ▶

The development of building skills in the sixteenth century resulted in the construction of ceilings, of larger, often stained-glass, windows and, eventually, of two-storey houses. Although much of the decoration of extant Tudor houses is now lost, interior surfaces were characteristically brightly painted. Ceilings, wood panelling, doorways and fireplaces were covered with ornate designs, typically incorporating the scrolled shapes of strapwork motifs on a gold background. Rooms were more elaborately furnished, and brightly coloured needlework and woven cloths were used as drapes and hangings, and also as integral upholstery.

Rich, deep colours are
replaced by cooler,
restrained tones

▲ EARLY RENAISSANCE

The Renaissance began in Florence in the fourteenth
century with a fascination with the art and
architecture of classical antiquity. Wealthy patrons of
the arts such as Lorenzo de Medici ensured the
proliferation of the antique style, and cabinet-makers
and other craftsmen began to design items
specifically for domestic interiors for the first time.
Sumptuous furniture, rugs and tapestries facilitated
comfortable interiors, and walls and ceilings were
painted with lavish and colourful classical designs.

◄ HIGH RENAISSANCE

From the end of the fifteenth century, Renaissance
style was at its height, and the fashion spread to
Rome, Venice and, subsequently, throughout Italy
and Europe. The design of High Renaissance homes
was far in advance of that in the rest of Europe.
Villas were divided into individual rooms – halls,
anterooms, bedchambers and, significantly, long
galleries, used for exercise, conversation and the
display of treasures and fine paintings. The functional
concerns of previous interior decorators had been
replaced with a regard for elegant proportions and
styles and a more restrained use of colour.

The 17th and 18th centuries in Europe

BAROQUE ▼ ▶

Baroque style of the seventeenth and eighteenth centuries was dramatic and ornate, with a grandeur and exuberance suitable for rich palaces and imposing Catholic churches. It is seen in all its excess in Louis XIV's massive palace of Versailles, where copious gilding and mirror glass is backed by scarlet fabric-lined walls and sumptuous tapestries produced by his Gobelins factory. Baroque colours were rich and royal – bright purple, emerald green, sapphire blue and deep yellow. English Baroque, never as extreme as its European counterparts, can be seen in Sir Christopher Wren's St.Paul's Cathedral and at Blenheim Palace, Sir John Vanbrugh's masterpiece.

◄ ROCOCO

The Rococo style flourished in France, southern Germany and Austria during the first half of the eighteenth century. More delicate and playful than the Baroque, Rococo designs were on a smaller scale, designed for domestic interior decoration. An appealing palette of light colours – pale pink, apple green, sky blue and apricot – is characteristic of the Rococo style. Ornamentation was provided by scroll and shell work, intricate plaster mouldings, glass chandeliers, mirrors and delicate porcelain. The pale colours and reflective surfaces created light and airy rooms in which the gentle and witty frivolities of the age could be pursued.

Classical revival in the 18th and 19th centuries

NEO-CLASSICAL

In mid-eighteenth-century Rome, Neo-classicism represented a reaction to the over-elaboration of the Baroque and Rococo styles. It was stimulated by a new interest in the antique, prompted by the archaeological discoveries at Pompeii and Herculaneum. The Neo-classical colour palette consisted of tones of white and grey, bright primary colours and accents of black and gold. This was an era of grand, elegant formality, and the Neo-classical style spread across Europe and America, persisting into the nineteenth century. In England, architect Robert Adam developed a refined Neo-classicism, using a palette of pale green, blue and pink.

FRENCH EMPIRE ▶

The Empire style originated in the 1790s and became fashionable in Paris during the early nineteenth century. It shared many of the Greek and Roman decorative elements of Neo-classicism, but also incorporated an interest in Egyptian motifs, such as the sphinx and the winged lion, as a result of Napoleon's Egyptian campaigns. Rooms were tented in military style with brilliantly coloured silks, and other fabrics were generously swagged. Walls might also be lined with pleated silk of bright yellow, green or crimson, or decorated with scenic wallpapers. Furniture was on a grand scale, decorated with gilding and ormolu, often with legs in animal forms.

Antique colours
are derived from
the great ancient
civilizations

SWEDISH EMPIRE ▲

Neo-classicism spread across Europe during the late
eighteenth and early nineteenth centuries, and
Sweden developed its own interpretation of the
Empire style. Also known as Gustavian, after the
reigning monarch, Swedish Empire was a
harmonious and highly decorative style that
successfully balanced rustic simplicity and elegant
sophistication. Natural or white-painted woods are
characteristically used with carved gilt mouldings and
delicately stencilled friezes to create airy and light
classical interiors. The colours of the Swedish Empire
style are softer than those used elsewhere in Europe
during this period – white, grey, blue, green and

Britain and America in the 18th century

GEORGIAN ▲

The Georgian style of architecture and decoration spanned more than a century, from 1714–1830. It was characterized by a well-proportioned, classical elegance and restraint – evident, for example, in the symmetrical use of twelve-paned sash windows and carefully calculated wall divisions and carved mouldings. Robert Adam dominated interior design in the late eighteenth century, popularizing pale shades of blue, pink and green. The later Georgian palette was even cooler: cream, grey, the palest greens and yellows became popular.

Colour defines
elegant architecture
and furniture

COLONIAL AMERICAN ▲

Colonial style in America spans a long period, from the mid-seventeenth century up to the time of the Declaration of Independence in 1776. Broadly speaking, Colonial design is informal and rustic, drawing upon a mixture of British and local folk art ideas. Towards the end of the period, interior decoration began to have a distinctly American look. Classical principles were pared down to create less ornamented interiors, furnished with well-made provincial wooden furniture. Paint colours were produced using local pigments, creating strong, matt, earthy shades of brown, cream, ochre, blue and dull red. Pigment was sometimes mixed with milk to make pastel shades. Stencilling on walls and furniture was the dominant decorative device.

Britain and America in the early 19th century

REGENCY ▼ ▶

Regency design in the early years of the nineteenth century in Britain was of a heavier Neo-classicism than that of the elegant Georgian style. Interior motifs were inspired by strict Ancient Greek, Roman and Egyptian forms. Wall surfaces were often broken up with paint effects, or with small stencilled or freehand-painted patterns. Regency colours were darker and more flamboyant than earlier palettes – vivid blues, greens and reds, for example, were thrown into relief with white or cream detailing.

Intense and daring
shades are highlighted
with white

AMERICAN FEDERAL ▲

Federal style – inspired, in part, by French Empire and British Regency counterparts – flourished in America at the end of the eighteenth and start of the nineteenth century. The style has more delicacy than the Colonial forms that preceded it, and is simpler and more restrained than contemporary European designs, although furniture and window dressings – with gracefully swagged curtains – were still influenced by European models. Intense shades of blue, green and mustard are typical of the Federal colour palette, complemented by subtle, muted shades of lavender and neutral creams and greys. These were painted, increasingly, on to smoothly plastered, rather than panelled, walls.

The second half of the 19th century

GOTHIC REVIVAL ▼ ▶

Mid-nineteenth-century Romanticism inspired an interest in medieval art and architecture, particularly for the elaborate, ecclesiastical styles of the Gothic period. Furniture designer and architect A. W. N. Pugin was an influential advocate of the Gothic Revival, taking charge of the Medieval Court at the Great Exhibition of 1851. The designs and colours of the Gothic Revival are strong and dramatic. Deep reds, greens and yellows formed the base of a rich colour palette for heavy textured fabrics, and contrasted with the dark tones of solid oak furniture and rough pewter and silver accessories.

▲ Victorian

Victorian interiors were characteristically full of pattern, cluttered with elaborate ornaments and accessories and draped with fabric, in stark contrast to the elegant Georgian and Regency rooms that they succeeded. Industrial prosperity meant that people wanted to show off their new status and wealth and exploit new-found opportunities for comfort and secure family life. Walls were generally papered with elaborate designs, and woodwork was darkly painted or grained. Deep, rich colours – reds, greens, purples – were opulent and even gaudy.

◄ Art Nouveau

The Art Nouveau period spanned only the last eight years of the nineteenth century, but it sowed the seeds of modern design, taking no historical precedent and achieving an enduring appeal. Originating in France, the style swept across Europe and America. Designs were characterized by curving, stylized, naturalistic motifs, and interior decorating colours were light and atmospheric – pink, blue, mauve and yellow contrasted strongly with black, white or grey in spirited combinations.

Britain at the turn of the century

ARTS AND CRAFTS ▼

The influence of William Morris and his disciples in the second half of the nineteenth century upon British styles of decoration was pervasive. Favouring hand-crafted, traditional manufacture above machine technology, he laid the foundations for an austere and simple style of decoration that persisted into the twentieth century. The oppressive, dark colours of the Victorian palette were rejected in favour of lighter, natural colours. The Arts and Crafts period saw a return to earthy browns, ochres, rusts and greens that provided the painted background to simple wooden furniture made from oak and other native woods. Leather upholstery, simple curtains and pewter and brass accessorized the style.

Natural and pale
colours let light
into interiors

EDWARDIAN ▲

By the early years of the twentieth century, British interiors were notably simpler than the elaborate Victorian rooms that preceded them. The Edwardians lived in smaller houses than those of their parents, and created a lighter, more spacious interior style as a result. Elegant classical styles of furniture once more came into vogue, enhanced by pale paint colours and delicately patterned and tinted wallpapers. White and pastel shades were chosen in contrast to heavy Victorian colours and in keeping with the desire for airy and bright rooms bathed in natural daylight. Pale green, blue, yellow, apricot and mauve were used with white or cream for woodwork to create relaxed and calm decoration.

Modern styles for the 20th century

ART DECO ▶

The twentieth century was in the grip of the machine
– mass production of goods was now possible, and
everything, including transport, was faster and more
streamlined. The Art Deco style, named long after
but deriving its snappy title from the 1925 Paris
exhibition of decorative arts, was a celebration of the
glamour and innovations of the age. Its decorative
inspiration was a heady mix of contemporary events
– Cubism, the shocking new creations of the Russian
ballet, the Egyptian treasures revealed in
Tutankhamen's tomb, the ancient art of Central
America, the shapes of steam liners and motor cars.
Its new materials were glass, chrome and lacquer,
pale woods and linoleum. Not surprisingly, the style
was realized with exotic, shocking new colours –
lime green, purple and brilliant orange, contrasted
with black, white and silver.

A brilliant

primary palette

is new and fun

Modernism ▲

Twentieth-century modernism is a catch-all phrase,
denoting emerging styles that were realized in
different ways and at different times. In Britain,
modernism is most closely associated with styles
conceived in the 1930s and adapted to the utilitarian
needs of the 1940s, which emerged properly after
the Second World War. The 1950s heralded the start
of mass-produced, contemporary design as we know
it today. For the first time, home decoration was fun
and bright. Colours ranged from bright pinks,
oranges and greens to ice-cream pastels.

From psychedelia to a new naturalism

SWINGING SIXTIES ▶

The social changes of the 1960s were reflected in daring new designs and colours for interiors. A consumer culture, home technology and suburbia all influenced a style that was as much about a way of life as it was an aesthetic. The youth market exploded in the 1960s and interior design catered to a generation that wanted to dissociate itself from the past – and from its parents. The bright primary colours of Pop Art and psychedelia and the distracting patterns of Op Art emerged in fake animal skins, abstract posters and comic-book images, combined with plastic furniture and fittings and vinyl flooring. Space-age moulded chairs, lava lamps, low-slung sofas and glass tables were carefully positioned in white-painted rooms. Colours were not only bright, they were also fluorescent, mixed in deliberately unnerving combinations, such as fuchsia pink with mustard yellow or fluorescent green with brilliant purple.

◄ TWENTY-FIRST-CENTURY LIVING

The twentieth century interior moved on at
technological speed, absorbing the high-tech styles
of the 1970s, the reactionary excesses of the 1980s
and a decorative backlash in the 1990s that tokened
a new concern for the environment and for a simpler
way of living. In the closing decades, minimalism
rubbed shoulders with country chintz, and new
synthetics were sold alongside seagrass mats and
natural linen curtains. At the start of the twenty-first
century, regard for the environment (albeit confused)
has seen a substantial return to the use of natural
materials for home decoration, and with it has come
a restrained colour palette of tonal creams, beiges
and browns in every gradation. We demand
significantly more of our interior spaces than our
forefathers – functionality is taken for granted, and
they must now feed us body and soul and,
increasingly, become our work areas, too. In such an
environment, personality colours find their place.

Further Reading

Personality theory and colour

Bonds, Lilian Verner, *Colour Healing*, London, 1994
Chiazzari, Suzy, *The Healing Home*, London, 1998
Eiseman, Leatrice, *Colours for Your Every Mood*, New York, 1998
Itten, Johannes, *The Elements of Colour*, London, 1970
Sun, Howard & Dorothy, *Colour Your Life*, London, 1992
Warrender, Carolyn, *Carolyn Warrender's Book of Colour Scheming*,
    London, 1996
Westgate, Alice, *Home Colour Directory*, London, 1999
Wright, Angela, *The Beginner's Guide to Colour Psychology*,
    London, 1995

Interior design

Barnard, Julia & Nicholas, *New Decorator*, London, 1999
Gilliatt, Mary, *Period Decorating*, London, 1990
Gore, Alan & Ann, *The History of English Interiors*, Oxford, 1991
Innes, Jocasta, *Paint Magic* (revised edition), London, 2000
Miller, Judith & Martin, *Period Style*, London, 1989
Miller, Judith, *Classical Style*, London, 1998
Miller, Judith, *Colour*, London, 2000
Sloan, Annie & Gwynn, Kate, *Colour in Decoration*, London, 1990
Warrender, Carolyn, *Carolyn Warrender's Decorating Course*,
    London, 1999

Services and Workshops

Pennie Cullen

Workshops on the use of colour in the home, as outlined in this book, are arranged through Growing Colour. Organized in small groups, the workshops increase knowledge of the use of colour to decorate the home or the office.
Apply in writing to:
Growing Colour, Stable Cottage, Lady Oak Lane, Bedgebury Cross, Goudhurst, Kent TN17 2RD, enclosing a s.a.e.
(tel and fax 01580 211728;
e-mail growingcolour@cullen-and.co.uk).

Consultancy services to private clients and businesses, including MBTI personality tests and workshops, are occasionally available on application to the above address.

Collaboration with a paint manufacturer enables Growing Colour to give concrete advice on seasonal paints for home and business environments.

Carolyn Warrender

Workshops on colour scheming teach how to choose and co-ordinate personalized colours to give your home an individual and professional look. Stencilling workshops include all the techniques necessary to decorate walls, floors, fabrics and furniture.
For details, send a s.a.e. to:
Carolyn Warrender Design, PO Box 108,
Chipping Norton D. O., Oxon OX7 4PU
(tel 01608 677285; fax 01608 677295;
e-mail carolynwarrender@lineone.net).

Available by mail order from Carolyn Warrender Design:
Colour Scheming and Interior Design home decoration packs and stencil kits and accessories. Send a s.a.e. to the above address for details.

Carolyn Warrender Design also undertakes interior design contracts, interior design/colour staff training, retail consultancy and lectures on interior design, colour and furnishing design development.

ANSWERS TO QUESTIONNAIRE ON PAGES 70–71

Add up your a, b, c, and d choices. The letter you scored most indicates the season and personality type you are likely to be:

a	Spring	c	Autumn
b	Summer	d	Winter

An individual's personality will often reveal traits from several seasons. If your score was similar for two seasons, your dominant type will be the season you relate most to when studying the individual characteristics in closer detail.

Index

Numbers in *italics* refer to illustrations

Authors' Acknowledgments

Both authors would like to thank everyone at Frances Lincoln – our editor, designer and picture researcher – for all their input and hard work. Thanks also to Colefax & Fowler, Woodstock Furniture, Brookmans Design Group of Sheffield and all the picture libraries that have provided photographs. In particular, many thanks to Karen Howes of The Interior Archive.

Many people have contributed to the theories and background of this book, through their own books, through courses and by advising us. They are too many to mention all by name. Pennie Cullen would like to give special thanks to Pamela Allsop and to Angela Wright of Colour Affects. The colour courses run by the International Association of Colour were very instructive, as were visits to the colour units at The South Bank University and Derby University.

Picture Acknowledgments

a=above, *b*=below, *l*=left, *r*=right

Peter Anderson © FLL (designer Carolyn Warrender) 11, 48, 54*al*, 54*ar*, 62, 100–101

Arcaid/Richard Bryant 117*l* (Hancock Shaker Village), 132*r* (architect Tsao & McKown), 139 (architect Katie Bassford-King, designed by Touch Interior Design), 142*ar* & 155 (Pingree House, Salem, Massachusetts), 147*a*, 147*b* (Villa di Maser, Treviso); Lucinda Lambton 146*b*, 149 & 157*a*; Richard Waite 162 (designer Jane Collins)

Axiom/ Chris Caldicott 144; James Morris 49 (architect James Gorst); Peter Wilson 156

Brookmans Design Group, Sheffield 36

Chris Caldicott 93*r*

Christopher Drake © FLL 41, 77*b*, 86–87, 105*r*, 108–109, 151

Andreas von Einsiedel 32*al* & 52 (designers Gordana & Peter Tyler), 34*ar* & 42 (Heather Weaver, Guinevere Antiques), 34*br* & 40*a* (designers Gordana & Peter Tyler), 39 (designer Tara Bernard), 43 (designer Grant White), 47*b* (designer Michael Reeves), 56 (designer Kelly Hoppen), 59 (designer Lester Bennett), 66*bl* & 107*r* (designer M. Antonin), 69 (designers Anders & Tammy Christiansen), 77*a* (designer Grant White), 85*r* (designer Frédéric Méchiche), 106*a* (designer M. Antonin), 111*a* (designer Monica Apponyi), 136*r* (designer Frédéric Méchiche)

Polly Farquharson © FLL 158 (Kelmscott Manor)

Tim Imrie © FLL 123*l* (designer John Sutcliffe)

The Interior Archive/Tim Beddow 118*a* (designer Dominique Kieffer); Fernando Bengoechea 76*a*, 128–129, 134*a* (designer Chessy Rayner); Nicolas Bruant 148; Ken Hayden 50–51 (designer Jonathan Reed), 140*b* (designer Jonathan Reed); Cecilia Innes 1 (architect Yturbe), 14*br* (architect Manolo Mestre); Simon McBride 2 & 110, 120*r* & 121*r*, 122*a* & 123*r*; James Mortimer 142*bl* & 161 (architect Le Corbusier); Fritz von der Schulenburg 8–9*al*, 34*bl* & 46, 38 (architect Jean Oh), 40*b*, 57 (designer Mimmi O'Connell), 74, 75 (designer Jasper Conran), 78*a*, 78–79*b* (Barry Ferguson), 95*b* (designer Bunny Williams), 102*a* (architect Jean Oh), 103 (Hill House, Charles Renny Mackintosh), 104*b* (designer Miranda Humphries), 137*l*, 142*al* & 152, 145 (architect Schinckel), 150*a* (Pavlosk, St Petersburg), 157*b* (Liberty), 159 (Laureston Castle); Thomas Stewart

88*b*, Christopher Simon Sykes 146*a*; Simon Upton 10, 44 (designer Colefax & Fowler), 84*b* (designer Ilaria Miani), 107*l* (designer Ilaria Miani), 141*r* (designer David Hare), 154 (Geoffrye Museum); Wayne Vincent 60; Andrew Wood 8–9*bl*, 9*br*, 12 (designer Nicholas Haslam), 33 (artist Arabella Johnson), 76*b* (designer Christine Rucker, The White Company), 79 (designer Osborne & Little), 119*l* (designer Stephanie Hoppen), 140*a* (designer Kelly Hoppen); Edina van der Wyck 54*b* (The Rug Company), 63 (designer Atlanta Bartlett); Herbert Ypma 5 & 117*r*

Patrick McLeavey © FLL 4, 17

Antonio Maniscalco 105*l*

Narratives/Jan Baldwin 53, 55 (Roger Oates Design), 111*b*, 133*l*; Polly Wreford 14*ar* & 21

Michael Paul 14*bl* & 31 (also background to 22–29 & 33), 91*l*, 93*l*, 112–113, 127*b*, 138*l* (The Hempel Hotel, London)

Alex Ramsay 14*al* & 30

Red Cover/Mark Bolton 95*a*; Andreas von Einsiedel 66*ar*, 85*l* (designer Frédéric Méchiche), 90*a* & 91*r*; Brian Harrison 118*b* & 119*r*; Ken Hayden 142*br* & 163; Winifried Heinze 66*br* & 138*r*; Andrew Twort 126–127*a*

Gary Rogers 116*b*

Ianthe Ruthven 45, 94, 96–97, 106*b*, 150*b*, 153

Paul Ryan/International Interiors 13 (designers Pryke & Romanuik), 61 (designers Pryke & Romanuik), 66*al* & 121*l* (designer Caroline Breet), 80–81 (designer Frances Halliday), 88*a* & 89*r* (designer Rob Bryant), 89*l* (designer Jan des Bouvrie), 104*a*, 120*l* (designer Gerry Nelissen)

Deidi von Schaewen 58, 132*l* & 133*r*, 141*l*

Simon Upton © FLL 125

Elizabeth Whiting and Associates 84*a*, 134*b* & 135*r*, 136*l*; Michael Dunne 18; Andreas von Einsiedel 65, 116*a*; Tim Imrie 137*r*; Di Lewis 47*a*, 122*b*, 135*l*; Spike Powell 102*b*, 160; Tim Street Porter 64, 90*b*, 92*a*, 92*b*; Simon Upton 124*b*

Woodstock Furniture 9*ar*

Publishers' Acknowledgments

The Publishers would like to thank Patrick McLeavey for designing the book, Judy Spours for editing the text, Zoë Carroll for editorial assistance and Marie Lorimer for the index.